AGENTS OF ECONOMIC DEVELOPMENT

An Essential Guide for Navigating Good, Bad, & Uncertain Times

Neal Wade &
William C. Smith

DEDICATION AND ACKNOWLEDGMENTS

Neal

Life is full of career twists and turns decorated with people who were pivotal at each juncture. Forty + years ago Sen. Sid McDonald asked me to run his gubernatorial campaign; followed by Steve Bradley, who brought me to Alabama Power and a wonderful fifteen years; the company's president Elmer Harris thought I should leave corporate life and enter a new profession as head of the Economic Development Partnership of Alabama; ten years later Peter Rummel expanded my economic development vision through a short stint at Florida's St. Joe Company; Gov. Bob Riley brought me back to Alabama as his chief economic development officer; and University of Alabama's president Dr. Judy Bonner saw through me the potential to create a university economic development academy which became the foundation of a four-university led national Advanced Economic Development Leadership professional development program. And through all these connected paths my wife, Mary Ann, a selfless volunteer, tap dancer extraordinaire, and impact player in her own right, has been a rock of support. William Cowper's 1774 poem says it best "God moves in a mysterious way His wonders to perform."

Now to the future – this book is dedicated to grandchildren Kylie, Macy, Morgan, Madison, Ragan, Layne, Austin and great grandchildren Jack, Elle, and Carson, all future agents of economic development.

Bill
This book is dedicated to my family – My wife Ginger and our four children: Jack, Lisa, Clay, and Ginny, six grandchildren, and five great-grandchildren. Ginger deserves the most credit. She encouraged me to pursue the career of my dreams.

Special recognition goes to the people who first introduced me to Economic Development many years ago, Dr. Ron Swager, Robert Ingram, and David Rumbarger.

I also want to thank my students who were willing to do the work it took to learn, the executives who believed in the value of first understanding the people you want to influence to achieve their individual and organizational goals, and all the people who serve their communities by participating in the work required to improve a community's economic base. What better job description is there than improving the quality of life and increasing the wealth of the people you serve?

Cover Image: *Large Group of People Moving to the Center* was licensed at DepositPhotos. https://depositphotos.com/home.html. It was a perfect image for *Agents of Economic Development* because it represents what must happen for a community to become a High Definition Community. For many communities, the best way to face these uncertain times.

A narrative runs throughout the book about an economic development organization in a town called Bedford. Both are fictional.

TABLE OF CONTENTS

INTRODUCTION

"Mayors, legislators, {economic developers} and elected leaders of every city, town, and village on the Earth must realize that every decision they make should consider the impact, first and foremost, on new jobs. The jobs war is what should get city leaders (and economic developers) up in the morning, what they should do all day, and what should keep them from getting to sleep at night."
—Jim Clifton, *The Coming Jobs War*

Who would have known when *The Coming Jobs War* was written in 2011 that America would experience one of its greatest economic swings in history. From the lowest national unemployment in more than fifty years to a worldwide pandemic that would claim countless lives multiplied by many more jobs.

As *Agents of Economic Development* is published, professional economic developers, elected officials, and community leaders are struggling with the pandemic aftermath and the important role creating jobs and sustaining existing jobs has on the recovery. Those who go to work every day as professional economic developers will move to the front lines in helping urban and rural communities

1

decide what actions must be taken to thrive or, in too many cases, just survive.

The principles outlined throughout the book stand the test of time and economic swings. There are lessons for each of the *Agents of Economic Development*: the volunteer leaders, elected officials, and, of course, the men and women who go to work every day, losing precious sleep, drinking too much coffee, and working tirelessly to grow and sustain jobs in their part of the world.

Throughout, these pages sound a recurring theme: Either lead, convene, or support, but, for heaven's sake, don't sit on the sidelines. Once agents, new to being involved in economic development, clearly understand that their jobs impact the well-being, pocketbooks, and future of so many of their community families, they will never approach their jobs the same again.

As Jim Clifton wrote so beautifully, creating jobs is "...what should get {us} up in the morning, what we should do all day, and what should keep us from getting to sleep at night."[1] This holds true now, more than ever.

As you will read in the last chapter, economic development is not a task that you finish. Former Tennessee basketball Coach Pat Summitt wrote about success in her book *Reach for the Summit* – "Success is a project that's always under construction. Somehow, you have to commit to get better every day, no matter how successful you were the day before."[2]

The timeliness of *Agents* underscores how true Coach Summit's statement is. Yesterday, it was easier to recruit a new project, help an entrepreneur create a new company, or assist an existing industry expansion. But today, the ground underneath our feet shakes because it is not as easy to be on the front lines of job creation.

---

1 Jim Clifton, *The Coming Jobs War*, Gallup Press, 2011

2 Pat Summitt with Sally Jenkins, *Reach for the Summit*, 1998, Random House, NY.

Tomorrow our world will change again and so will the way we approach our tasks.

The beauty of being an agent of economic development lies in the outcomes our actions can have on the people we serve. Every day we walk into the office facing new, and often exciting, challenges with opportunities to significantly impact our little corner of the world.

This book was written for professional economic developers, elected officials, and all the citizens wanting to become involved in improving their community's standard of living. Each of you forms the team required to achieve economic success. Together you can, and do, make a difference in the lives of the people you serve through your tireless work and volunteer efforts.

Albert Einstein wrote that "...education is not the learning of facts, but the training of the mind to think."

If we've done our jobs correctly as authors, *Agents of Economic Development* will make you think and will help you examine how you approach your role as a professional, an elected official, and a leader who wants to see their community thrive. Thank goodness, it's not a textbook but a lively journey through this often misunderstood profession. Enjoy the trip and recognize that you will never arrive at the final destination because learning and varied experiences never stop.

CHAPTER 1

CHANGE AGENTS IN TURBULENT TIMES

"Unless you try to do something beyond what you have already mastered, you will never grow"
—Ralph Waldo Emerson

The Bedford mayor walked into the Wee Diner as the usual locals were again enjoying coffee, eggs, and the issues of the day following the several months all inside eating establishments were closed because of the pandemic.

"Good morning your honor," chimed one veteran of the diner's famous early morning round table. "We sure have missed our morning discussions and solving all the problems of the day."

Just two years ago, the group was riding the mayor about whether Bedford would bid on the HQ2 project knowing full well that Bedford didn't come close to the project criteria. Now, they were questioning how Bedford was going to recover after such a devastating impact on a medium-sized community.

Much of the nation was drifting toward recession and the pressure was on every elected official because citizens were really feeling the pinch. As the mayor sat down among the group of retired and the few still-working locals, he heard the elderly lawyer John Durbin ask the rhetorical question "What are you going to do to get our economy moving again? Where's economic development and jobs when we need it, especially now?"

Trying to be optimistic but not revealing too much, the mayor just said that there were things in the works that would be good for Bedford. Finally, the conversation moved to the resumption of football in just a few weeks. Nothing changes the subject better than sports and particularly high school football.

The mayor soon joined the ones leaving and immediately headed a couple of blocks straight for the Economic Development Agency (EDA)[3]. It was a glorious summer day and David McMillian was already at his desk as was his custom for an early start on the day.

David was starting his fifth year in Bedford and with the HQ2 project pressures in the past, but the unprecedented Coronavirus pandemic raging, he felt as if he'd been in the job for years. While he still had nice brown hair, he could see grey flakes sneak into his sideburns.

David heard the front door open as the mayor walked through the paneled hallway straight to the director's office.

"David, what are your ideas about how to address the virus aftermath?' said the slightly out of breath mayor. "Your big project isn't enough of a solution, especially since we might not win or it may get delayed because of the turbulence. We need a plan."

David sort of chuckled and said every mayor in America is asking that same question this morning. The pandemic had interrupted everything – small business, manufacturing, schools, churches, projects. And economic developers were now on the front line of recovery.

"Mayor, as you know, we've been working with other local organizations and our EDA board on a short, mid, and long-term

---

3 EDA and EDO (economic development organization) are used interchangeably throughout the book because both are extensively used in practice.

recovery plan," replied David. "It's still requires some finishing touches before show time but we're close. For once, it has brought all the players together for one cause – restoring Bedford's economy and getting businesses and industries back operating."

"Well, I don't want to be second-guessed for not focusing enough on recovery," said a clearly frustrated mayor. "Election time will be here in a few months and my opposition might question my lack of planning and aggression."

David chose his next words carefully and again reminded the mayor that the recovery team was almost ready to report to the Council and winning Project Penguin was also the agency's top priority. David knew both were testing his small staff as never before and, as the mayor left, he began to think through the day's meetings and what other challenges might surface.

As he strolled down the hall to convene a planning meeting for Project Penguin, he wondered how his colleagues across the country would spend their day as America faced a new normal.

Modern economic development in the United States may have begun with Henry Ford's growing automotive empire as new and larger assembly plants sprang up in Michigan just after the turn of the Twentieth Century. Certainly, it took professional root with the emergence of the Fantus Factory Locating Service in 1934.

In 1919, Felix Fantus began giving advice about land, buildings, transportation, utilities, local wages, and taxes following a site location search that moved his chair manufacturing plant from Chicago to Indiana. In the beginning, Fantus was not charging for all this "valuable" guidance but his son-in-law, Leonard Yaseen, thought their advice and professional guidance were worth a fee.

Young Yaseen couldn't convince his father-in-law to turn it into a business, so he left Chicago for New York in 1934. With his father-in-law's blessing, Yaseen opened his own consulting service, later known as the Fantus Factory Locating Service. The business muddled along through World War II but expanded into a multi-faceted organization as the country boomed following the war's end. With servicemen returning from the war and factories returning to normal operations, Fantus began advising cities, states, regions, and companies on how to relocate or attract expanding businesses to their areas.

For several decades, Fantus dominated the site location consulting business as numerous factories began moving out of the Northeast and Midwest to the rapidly growing industrial and less-costly South. By the time Yaseen retired, the company claimed to have engineered more than 4,000 expansions and relocations. [4]

With the economy booming and companies growing across America, Fantus' consulting spawned numerous professional companies. In fact, some of today's senior site consultant statesmen are Fantus alumni.

Economic Development Has and Is Evolving

The past couple of decades have seen an evolution for economic development mainly because of the onslaught of new technology and the sophistication of both site decision-makers and the professional economic developer. Almost everyone in and surrounding the profession is predicting an even greater change in the economic development process over the next decade and beyond as the use of artificial intelligence, necessary human skills, and society transform work.

---

4 Compiled from: *Ady Advantage,* July 1, 2019, Janet Ady, *As I See It - Site Selection Industry Marks its Centennial* – Part 1 of 2. https://adyadvantage.com/as-i-see-it-site-selection-industry-marks-its-centennial-part-1-of-2-the-early-years/

All this change brings an opportunity to reinforce/change your existing position or build a new position in decision-makers' minds. Woe unto those communities that do not look to the future and keep up! Remember, your competitors are not encumbered with how things are done now. They can take advantage of the opportunity to design their approaches to fit what prospects/consultants are currently seeking.

Successful EDAs have already begun to modify their strategies beyond the still main focus of attracting new industry. These professionals realized economic strengthening is best achieved through a broad-based job creation approach including attention to existing industry cultivation/expansion/retention, innovation/entrepreneurship, retail/commercial, and workforce/education development. This effort includes strengthening partnerships based upon strong, positive relationships throughout the community and ally network. Partners, also known as Force Multipliers,[5] include City, County, State officials, Region, Utilities, Real Estate, and other Economic Development Professionals, etc.

In every community, elected officials and volunteer leaders play a significant role in the job creation process. Decisions they make have a significant impact on the appeal, or lack thereof, of their communities to all types of businesses and the people they employ. Years ago, the advertising agency Saatchi & Saatchi[6] stated, "People want to locate in a place they love beyond reason." Earlier generations located where they found a job they wanted and learned to love the community. Today's millennial

---

5 Force Multipliers are those individuals and organizations who expand the community's economic development organization's reach to influencers, expertise, and prospects; help fulfill prospect demands, and have the capability to multiply budgets.

6 Based on the book by Kevin Roberts, *Lovemarks: The Future Beyond Brands*, Power House Publishing, April 2004.

generation decides where they want to live and play first and then they find a job.[7]

Every community's objective is to create an environment that allows prospects, residents, and decision-makers to "...love a community beyond reason." Most communities *want* to take control of the trajectory of their economy by focusing on key decision points that are central to the new wealth creation and retention processes. Unfortunately, for many communities, especially America's heartland, and more rural areas, it is not entirely possible to control their trajectory without first making some hard, sober decisions. Focusing limited resources forces you to make choices, to set priorities, to choose what are the most important things you need to respond to, to achieve your community's definition of success. Which wealth creation option(s) is the best match (create, attract, retain, and/or expand business; change the community's brand)? This fast-changing business environment we face means all economic development professionals need to reassess the processes they follow to create community wealth.

Therefore, we can be certain transformation is a major part of the evolving economic development process. Innovation, technology, and artificial intelligence are disrupting manufacturing. Rural communities are feeling disruption through population decline and dwindling tax resources. Urban areas experience disruption, too, by failing to adapt, diversify their economies, and not preparing the workforce pipeline for what is coming. Communities cannot stop change but they can manage their response to the evolving environment by laying out an effective plan focused on action. Economic developers can also adapt and become change agent leaders in turbulent times. **Adaptation** works during stable periods but is critical now.

As the local environment changes, the professional economic developer can review how he/she thinks regarding success and

---

7   The effect of COVID – 19 on this trend is yet to be seen.

what it will look like in this new age - "…am I brave enough to try new things." The days of accepting the status quo while trying to be competitive are over. Moving forward, disruptive economic development is required for a community's success.

> *"Even the wisest among them were at a hopeless disadvantage, for their only guide to sorting it out – the only guide anyone ever has – was the past, and precedents are worse than useless when facing something entirely new."[8]*

Agents of Economic Development focuses on the key aspects of successful community economic development and the disruptive roles each should play today and beyond in growing and sustaining quality jobs. The word "disruptive" in this context relates to ideas or actions that radically change strategies that need altering. Disruption is stopping something from continuing *as usual* - changing the traditional way we think so that those engaged in job creation/retention can be as effective as possible.

A cornerstone of *Agents of Economic Development* is **application.** Maybe we should begin by determining what application is not. It is not just accumulating knowledge. Understanding economic development precepts is just the beginning of the process. Application is putting into practice the knowledge we have accumulated and answering the question, "Now that we know this, So What?" What do we do with this knowledge and experience?

Throughout the Book of Proverbs, Solomon reminds us that the goal is to attain and apply wisdom. As you read *Agents of Economic Development,* the goal is that you grasp each section and determine the intentional application for your life, profession, and community.

---

8 William Manchester, *A World Lit Only by Fire,* about the fifteenth century on the verge of the Renaissance.

A Mistaken Obituary

In 1888, Alfred Nobel, the rich Swedish chemist and founder of dynamite, had a rare chance to stare into a haunting mirror. Alfred's brother had just died, but the newspaper mistakenly ran the obit for Alfred Nobel instead of his brother. The obituary was headlined "The Merchant of Death Has Died." He had that rare chance to read his own obituary describing what people thought of him and decided to change his life's purpose. He took $9 million, which was a huge amount of money then[9] and created the Nobel Peace Prize.[10]

Those involved in economic development, both directly and indirectly, have a rare opportunity to direct their life's purpose in the pursuit of improving the lives of those around us. The first time an employee at a recently opened or expanding manufacturing plant or local technology startup walks up to you with a bear hug in appreciation for their job, you will know the true impact economic development and specifically your work makes on the community.

Wise King Solomon in Proverbs 13:20 said, "He who walks with the wise grows wise...." As we walk through *Agents of Economic Development* the hope is to grow wise in the pursuit of job creation and new wealth for America's communities and take intentional steps to better our communities. It may be as an elected official, a professional economic developer, or an involved citizen, but it will take a concerted effort by communities, regions, and states to change and take advantage of your economy's trajectory.

---

9   Today a philanthropist would give an estimated, equivalent sum of $242,894,842. Number calculated on: https://www.officialdata.org

10   Kenne Fant, *Alfred Nobel: A Biography*, Arcade Publishing, 1991, Page 207.

CHAPTER 2
THE ECONOMIC DEVELOPMENT "CIRCLE OF LIFE"[11]

*"If you don't know where you are going
any road can take you there."*
—Lewis Carroll, Alice in Wonderland

"When you come to a fork in the road, take it!"
—Yogi Berra, Beloved Philosopher

*David walked into the small meeting room joining his staff as
they began Bedford's quest to win an elusive major manufacturing
project. Around the room sat his staff to begin their community's
quest to win an elusive major manufacturing project. For the past
long months, project activity had grinded to almost a halt, but
he had kept in touch with site consultants and target companies
throughout the turbulent stretch.*

*Bedford had received a RFP from one of the country's premier
site consultants three days ago and it was like a breath of fresh air.*

---

11 Music composed by Elton John, Lyrics by Tim Rice for The Walt Disney
Company movie, The Lion King, 1994.

David knew the consultant and they had Zoomed several times during the pandemic plus he had brought her into Bedford last year for a visit and round table with his community leadership team. David always "worked" as many site consultants as he could just to keep the network fresh but communications over the past long months had proved challenging. Every consultant was working from home so each contact needed to be worth the time for the consultant or it would boomerang on his approach.

Craig suggested as they walked toward the Penguin meeting that the EDA and Chamber should jointly convene a cross-section of existing businesses in Bedford to discuss impacts, possible action items, consequences to expect over the next eighteen months, possible revolving loan funds and any stimulus money that might be available. Craig suggested we should lead in convening this effort and take whatever appropriate roles would get the job done.

Just last year, the economic development agency completely re-worked its strategic marketing plan including a new website and social media campaign. While the words were never spoken, the economic development agency felt increased pressure by both private and government partners to produce. The pressure had only intensified with the dramatic economic downturn and many of Bedford's citizens needing work.

There were also unresolved tensions within the five-county regional alliance that included Bedford and it was understood that the member counties were working both sides of the street – supporting the regional initiative but covering their bases with intense local efforts. If David heard "you have to pull yourself up from your own bootstraps" once, he had heard it a hundred times. Maybe the Recovery Plan and Project Penguin were their chances to score big and quieten the naysayers.

David knew he had to get his mind focused on Project Penguin so, as everyone was settling in to hear the project specifics, David was grateful for a strong staff and supporting outside partners. Betsy

McCreary was his number two and the "real brains" in the outfit. Her mind was quick and her instincts even sharper. She had twenty years in the trenches and was content in her role and her own skin.

Craig Wood joined the staff two years ago and functioned as senior project manager. More organized and disciplined than David, he was fearless when it came to assembling the resources necessary to stay competitive in a project. He knew rarely, if ever, was a project won at the first sound of the bell and often reminded the group that this was a marathon, a process, not a sprint.

All three had completed various training courses but none had gone through college expecting to become economic developers. Just as every one of their peers, they had "backed into" the profession and OJT had prepared them for opportunities such as Project Penguin and challenges such as the Coronavirus.

Adrienne Jackson always sat between David and Betsy to make sure she did not miss any notes or assignments. She learned early on that every office needed a traffic cop who doubles as the office glue and Adrienne played that role to perfection. She was particularly interested in the recovery plan since her father-in-law was diagnosed positive but recovered after fourteen days quarantine. She was thankful that the job allowed her to focus on the community in a lead role and wanted to contribute any way she could. It was also good being back in the office face-to-face with her teammates even though they were social distancing.

Joining the small group was the EDA's volunteer chair Roger Barnett. He had moved up the volunteer ranks within the agency, so this drill was not new to him although he was about to find out that the stakes were much higher than previous projects, mainly because an economic jolt was so needed.

Roger had a successful financial consulting firm and was tied into the pulse of Bedford. With various community agencies working together on the pandemic recovery plan, the walls that over the years developed between agencies and governments were beginning to come down and Roger was seeing the kind of headway he knew was necessary to get everyone pulling together.

A deacon at his church, Craig was sitting in a middle seat almost in a posture of prayer. He reflected on the "team" practices that David had insisted on over the past year. Now, all would see if practice makes perfect.

For the next thirty minutes, Craig outlined the project with comments inserted about areas of strengths and weaknesses. Everyone chimed in as the clock moved closer to the lunch hour featuring sandwiches from David's favorite deli. As discussion, assignments, and lunch broke, the group headed toward their respective worlds reflecting on Project Penguin and pandemic recovery.

For decades the definition of economic development has evolved, changing both how and why we create and expand wealth. There may be as many definitions for economic development as stars in the universe, but all revolve around the process of creating new/increased wealth within a designated geographic area's economy. But when it's all broken down, it is a process of utilizing the known and sometimes unknown assets and resources in a community, state, or region to grow the economy. Do note, economic growth means a rise in real per capita income.

It may come as a surprise to some, but new wealth creation is much more than job recruitment or attraction. Too many believe the attraction of new industry is what economic development is all about. It certainly has always been the glamorous part given all the attention from the media – photos of people cutting ribbons, shovels scooping dirt, and front page/prominent news coverage. All too sexy to resist. However, even today's wise site consultants, who make much of their revenue from company recruitment, say that today's successful communities must focus their resources on the broad definition of job creation while creating a diverse local economy.

Therefore, the public benefits from the efforts of economic development organizations are more robust when the practitioners spend their time in each of the following target areas **in addition to industry attraction**[12]:

1. Cultivating/Retaining existing businesses,
2. Establishing an environment and infrastructure for entrepreneurs to make new discoveries, products, and technology,
3. Expanding the retail and commercial base to support the increased spending new jobs bring, and
4. Maybe more important than any of the others – developing a world-class education system that provides the talent pipeline necessary to fill new, expanding jobs while also sustaining existing employment. [13]

As each of these businesses and organizations prospers, the community will see rising wages and an improved standard of living. Each success contributes to an increase in the community's gravity – the ability to attract more attention to create and attract new business, as well as retain and expand existing business.

There is another important reason to use a broader definition and practice of economic development. The business world is in the beginning stages of rapid change. Previously, the pattern of economic development was relatively stable. Change was speeding up but proceeding in a somewhat predictable pattern because businesses were going through their normal, iterative planning processes. Aligning your activities with "what works" was easier to identify and deliver.

---

12 Each area requires resources and people's attention to prosper.
13 Firms buy machinery and technology. We humans require training on all this new technology.

Driven largely by technology, the effects of the pandemic, and the requisite workforce skills/aptitude needed, our future will be anything but stable. We must learn some new habits. Isolated technology effects are beginning to cause secondary orders of impact as change multiplies within and among adopting firms. This will only increase as entrepreneurs and existing businesses both strive to stay competitive by increasing the rate of innovation developed and utilized within their operations. Firms will also be looking to combine flexibility in their workforce and facilities. These changes mean communities and states must have the infrastructure necessary to prepare people to work in these new production environments. [14]

During the transition, economic development professionals and the diverse group of stakeholders must do what is necessary so their community will have a chance to help build the new economy. Remember, change brings opportunity. Your ability to adapt to the external change is best accomplished by paying attention to the signals coming from the market, especially from our selected targets and external circumstances (what is happening in the general economy). The market will send signals, e.g., robots able to teach themselves to learn a task and a skill. What are the implications for warehouses?

Thanks to the pandemic's disrupted global critical supply chains, U.S. firms are looking for more stability. Expect to see these U.S. firms move to more local sources: previously considered secondary to foreign sources, and to new local sources. Does your community have the necessary infrastructure and workforce to accommodate these new demands?

Other signals also exist. GE Aircraft division was able to build a one-piece fuel nozzle using 3D printing (additive manufacturing). Previously these nozzles used 18 different parts. The new single

---

14 For example, Alabama Robotic Technology Park.

part was also 25% lighter. What do you expect to happen to GE's existing supplier base as this process widens to cover more parts? Would it make more business sense for GE to build these parts themselves? Are any GE supplier plants located within your community? What will the outcome be on them?

The key is to recognize the signal and its potential effect early. **Build your strategy around learning**. The business world is at a point in time when the past cannot help us predict the future.[15] A focus on learning will enable you to adapt to change and act faster than your competition while also being less disruptive to your own organization, community, allies, and other stakeholders.

Technology, computers, and robots using machine learning to acquire a skill without human intervention will radically change how goods are manufactured and distributed as well as how humans interact with technology. The impact on industry, services, and the workforce mean our future will mimic the previous industrial revolution's pace of change when we left agriculture, moved to the cities, learned new skills, and worked in plants.

Professionals are recognizing that tech jobs will be driving economic development in the short-term as the demand for data analysts and engineers is expected to be robust. Also, of note, the Bureau of Labor Statistics predicts employment of math occupations is projected to **grow 26 percent** from 2018 to 2028, faster than any other occupation.[16]

What makes economic development so important for a community to support? Economic development's appeal flourished as engaged citizens became aware other communities were using

---

15 Business models work. Businesses adopt the model and refine it and finally pursue cost advantages because all the competitors are so similar. Then a disruptor appears and turns the old model upside down. Sam Walton revolutized department store retailing with WalMart. Jeff Bezos's Amazon did it again, even before the pandemic. The lesson is to pay attention to the signals.

16 *Occupational Handbook Outlook*, https://www.bls.gov/ooh/math/

economic development to improve their standard of living with higher wages and an improved quality of life. In fact, **Done Right** economic development is central to a vibrant, growing community.

It is important for all involved to understand that economic development is an investment, not an expense. Payback is not immediate but lasts well into the future as the community lays a foundation, then builds a growth-oriented economy. While you can see jumps in employment over the short-term, the best way to evaluate the return on a community's investment in economic development is over a longer period of time.

Mom and Apple Pie

We toss the term "economic development" around like a baseball. Every candidate running for office incorporates some form of economic development into their platform, making it equal to "mom and apple pie." Every day, it surfaces in the media in one form or another, either pro or con. Actually, the public is somewhat jaded by the term because they have heard it so much and in so many contexts.

However, a key characteristic of successful local economic development is that constituents substantially participate in the process of changing the fundamental structure of their local economy. Therefore, citizens must make the connection between a successful job creation/retention program and the resulting new wealth that trickles down throughout the community. Constituencies enjoy the benefits from the rise in per capita income but often the mental bridge is not complete for them to make the connection between active job creation and the resulting ripple effect of more disposable income without an active, vocal EDA.

In most cases, a dying community is devoid of successful job creation and the resulting trickle-down increase in disposable income. A dying community usually struggles with declining tax revenues impacting education, poverty, crime, and community spirit. Dying communities are normally losing population. In some communities, the moment you arrive in town you can sense the "downer atmosphere." With a deeper look into the numbers slide and the personal stories, there is a realization the community is facing serious economic vibrancy issues.

Far too many communities in America's heartland or the rural parts of the country are experiencing the negative effect of declining population and shrinking tax bases. For others, the long tentacles of successful job creation, additional tax revenue, and enhanced disposable income derived from new and expanded businesses, help struggling communities provide necessary infrastructure such as roads, parks, libraries, fire protection, police, and quality medical services. This isn't accomplished by magic but through a process. It's especially tough work as declining communities find it difficult to stop the bleeding.

A Major Shift

In today's economy, it is important to diversify the business base to reduce a community's vulnerability on a single or limited business sectors. Economic downturns often emphasize the need for diversification but too often the lessons do not remain in place when the local economy starts booming again – communities often revert to their sweet spot and what is best known.

For example, in the mid-twentieth century, many communities in the South depended heavily on textiles and agriculture as their primary wage providers and did not anticipate, in particular, a major shift in textile production. Some did not read the tea leaves signaling a mass exodus to less-expensive off-shore manufacturers and failed to diversify their economies enough to insulate against financial stagnation and, in some cases, collapse. Some communities have rebounded nicely, often with even better, higher-paying industrial, technological, entrepreneurial, and assembly replacements. Others are still struggling with declining economies and populations.

As this book is being completed, there is a national debate about the strength of the nation's economic recovery post-Coronavirus. The good news is the heightened attention to both urban and rural economies and how to emerge from one of history's most serious health and economic crisis.

Across the U.S. some cities can attack from a position of strength while others were already struggling from decades of population decline, economic stagnation, and jobs loss. Some are addressing the issues directly through innovative leadership, the tearing down of walls, creative approaches to reviving local economies, and convincing people that they can truly make a difference in their communities.

Revivals in motivated cities and communities are possible when all the right ingredients come together.

CHAPTER 3
PLAYING IS EVERYTHING

EDA board chairman Roger Barnett and his fellow board members had supported the organization's three-year planning process that helped define a broader role for the agency. The plan had included the traditional buffalo hunt for new companies but sustaining and creating jobs from existing industries were beginning to take a more center-stage in the action plan.

With the pandemic aftermath, focusing on existing industries, small businesses, and the previously growing retail sector now look like good strategies. Many small businesses were really suffering but the year-long intense effort focused on personally getting to know the businesses and their challenges, was paying off. Now follow up in the community's recovery phrase would be easier and, hopefully, yield some positive results.

Not a strong tourism area, the EDA also initiated bridges to the tourism agency and several of the key players. Together, they had begun a synchronized social media campaign defining the uniqueness of Bedford as a place to live, work, and play. Before the country shut down, the partnership was beginning to produce results as surveys indicated that business decision-makers often chose the lakes, hiking trails, and great golf courses around Bedford for family outings. So, a natural tie between the EDA and tourism was beginning to blossom. Now, they and others were sitting at the table desperately working on a community recovery plan.

Betsy McCreary had experienced the pendulum effect periodically during her two professional decades, first in government planning and then in economic development, but nothing like these past few months. Her career began in Bedford's city government in the planning department. But midway through her fifth year she longed for a change and backed into an opening at the EDA. Her research and data skills were a "God-send" to the agency, and she soon became indispensable.

Just like almost every economic development organization in the country, the focus was primarily about recruiting new companies because everyone knew elected officials loved announcements and the publicity generated from breaking ground for a new company. Too often, the competition model was simple – "What can you offer my project and how will you solve any problems I have?"

But times changed! Decisions became more data driven, often followed by the request by the company or site consultant to "prove it." At first, Bedford tried to "win" every project at the outset rather than understanding the elimination process that required communities to compete at each stage of the competition before being in a realistic position to win. They learned the hard but valuable lesson in the process that "Playing is Everything" as compared to "Winning is Everything." As Betsy said to her best friend, you must stay in the game long enough to be in a position to win.

Now everyone on the team would see with Project Penguin if all the practices, training, and staff assignments would pay off. In one week, they would need to deliver their initial response to Project Penguin and, hopefully, make the cut for a site visit.

Legendary Green Bay Packers coach Vince Lombardi once said that "Winning isn't everything – it's the only thing." That may be true in football, but not so much in economic development competition.

Economic development recruitment and existing industry retention are variations on the concept of winning. First, of course, you have to get in the game. Once that goal is accomplished, never assume a win but always believe that you *can* win if you are doing the things necessary to stay in the game. In the world of business retention and attracting new jobs, ***playing is everything!***

Economic development is the process of elimination, which forces communities/states to try to stay in the game long enough to make the **Final Few**. Then, in the championship series of the last decision, winning becomes the goal. The process is actually similar to the current college football playoff system. Teams are doing everything they can to make the final four and then the goal becomes winning the National Championship.

In reality, we cannot fully control the outcome, but we can control the focus devoted to the process. The focus should not be on winning a project and the victory lap – the focus should be on all the steps necessary to **stay in the competition** to the Final Few.

As the University of Alabama football Coach Nick Saban preaches to his staff, players, and assistants: *"Don't think about the SEC Championship, the National Championship, or even two games down the road. Think about what you need to do today, in this drill, in this exercise, in this game to be successful."*[17]

One site selection consultant said that he was not really a site selector but a site eliminator. He followed up by saying that often, a lot of "good" communities are eliminated in favor of better or "great" communities. The goal for any "good" community is to elevate their status to compete favorably in today's competitive job creation environment. However, Celine Dion cautioned her music

---

17 Constant Renewal, 2019 Newsletter, www.constantrenewal.com

students "you can't be good all the time – you have to be great when it's (the right) time."[18]

In the U.S. there are more than five thousand communities and economic development agencies chasing a few hundred quality projects each year. While the math makes it tough, successful communities find a way to increase their competitive odds until they are in earshot of the Final Few.

The Harvesting Process

It is said the hope of the human race is stored on the Norwegian island of Spitsbergen almost 800 miles from the North Pole. It is the Svalbard Global Seed Vault,[19] an underground storage facility for hundreds of thousands of seeds from tens of thousands of crop species from around the world. It is designed to be the source of seeds for replanting food crops in the aftermath of a global catastrophe.

Seeds and the planting of seeds represent the essence of life, and in our case, the essence of economic development prospecting. When a prospecting seed is planted, there is a season where nothing is visible from the surface. Although the seed's roots are beginning to sprout and dig into the soil, there is no life above the ground. Rootwork takes time and is aided by continued watering and nurturing; relationship building in the economic development process. Each type of seed, just as each economic development project, has a unique gestational period.

Understanding and embracing the gestation process in growing plants mirrors the process for economic development projects. Both frustrated and successful gardeners tell you it takes time, nurturing, and understanding the uniqueness of each plant. In addition, it is important for an economic development organization's volunteers and elected leaders to understand and embrace the

---

18 Celine Dion quoted on https://www.iamchrisjamison.com/179698/2017/3/22/season-12-the-battles-premiere

19 Svalbard Global Seed Vault, www.croptrust.org

process as well. With understanding, they can watch, encourage, and participate as the nurturing process takes hold and, hopefully, produces new wealth for the community.

Profiling – in a good way

Site selection consultants and companies seeking expansion locations profile communities every day. While the term is often not always politically correct or even proper in some circumstances, in site selection it is necessary for decision-makers to complete the selection process. Site eliminators, as they are known to some, must profile or determine how the communities under consideration rank on critical success factors:

- Access to certain infrastructure needs – many studies rank infrastructure as the number one criterion in the elimination process including e.g., internet bandwidth, utilities, logistics, etc.
- Product – available buildings, prepared/certified sites.
- Talent pool/pipeline availability and within what radius – usually a close second in the site selection importance ranking.
- Education status – graduation rates, industry credentials, apprenticeships, etc.
- Educational and research infrastructure – proximity to research universities.
- Fair and competitive variable operating costs – pay attention, this number can be changing due to automation.
- Business support services.
- Quality of life and amenities for families transferring from other locations.
- Competitive Incentive package – fair to taxpayers and the client company.
- Thoroughly aligned private and government local leadership.
- Reputation for service after the sale – has the community "...been there before **and delivered**?"

A summary of the critical success factors indicates it is all about mitigation or minimization of risks for the client as well as maximizing the opportunity for success. Or in the blunt words of one company executive, "Get me from spending money to making money the fastest possible way."

In today's business world, time is money so any way to shorten timelines and provide greater certainty will help mitigate risk factors. For instance, streamlining the permitting process so that the timing to get a building permit allows the construction timetable to proceed as quickly as possible.

Over-regulation can be a real drain on a company's profits and sends a signal that the state/community is more concerned about red tape than creating jobs. Perception is reality and reputations for not being business-friendly can quickly send your community or state to the sidelines – eliminated from consideration.

Be risk averse!

Absolutes to stay in the game

What are some suggestions and truisms for communities to stay in the game to the Final Few?

- Know your community backward and forward – warts and all. This truism is important because the prospect or site-eliminating consultant will probably know your community as well or better than you and challenge the warts that impact his/her project. Consultants are known for coming to a potential location a day early and asking the local restaurant's wait staff, "What is it like living here?". Community development is an important part of economic development. Get to know the people who will likely interact with your prospects – restaurant wait staff and hotel front-desk attendants. A growing local economy is in their interests too.

- Build a great local team – both the professional staff and the leadership team. While some might not want to admit it, but usually, communities win projects, not economic development agencies or a particular elected-official. The right leadership team for each project and the professional agency can make all the difference in the elimination process. A strong volunteer team and economic development agency professional staff are the lifeblood of the successful economic development organization. This is an area where leadership must pay attention in determining the strengths and diversity of the local team for each project.

- Prospect companies are looking for a professional approach which is all the more reason to prepare the staff, elected officials, and community leaders for those coveted in-person individual/corporate visit opportunities. **Listen** and learn from what the project team is saying, or not saying. Then prepare and react accordingly. Listening cannot be overemphasized, as there are always signals that can direct the community to focus on what is most important to the client/project. **Listen, be flexible, and adapt**. There is a reason the Good Lord gave us two eyes, two ears, and one mouth – to listen four times as much as we speak, especially early on in the process. Remember, the more the client speaks, the smarter you become. You will then be able to speak on what matters most to the people you want to influence.

- Know the prospect, the company, and the approach necessary to meet their needs. Please do not boilerplate from past presentations or RFPs – **make it unique** to each project. Focus on the company's objectives – react and solve their issues in a way that fits your community.

- Show confidence but not arrogance. Companies want to do business with communities they believe "...have been there before," understand the needs of a new business, show support for existing companies, and can deliver what has been promised. Note: If you make a promise to provide something to a prospect by a certain date, then keep your promise. If you cannot, then contact them on or before the agreed-upon date and let them know when you will have what they expect. People prefer working with those who keep them in the loop.

- Be sure the pipeline can deliver the talent promised. In today's project decisions, workforce availability is often the, or certainly a, key deciding factor. Decision-makers will most often require proof for your talent pipeline claims, emphasizing the importance, depth, and accuracy of your organization's research and data-driven information. Also, if the community delivers the required talent for a new company it will pay dividends when future prospect opportunities arise. Quite often, prospect decision-makers question existing companies on their local HR experiences. Existing industry success can sway the final decision a prospect makes about your community.

- The project needs to see your community as a **partner**, not a vendor. Final selection decisions are made on this very issue. Help the prospect see a successful future in your community through a professional and aligned community approach.

- Have fun! Oscar Wilde wrote, "Work is easy – fun is hard." Economic developers have the unique opportunity of coming to work every day and impacting individuals and their communities in ways most people can only imagine. Enjoy the journey!

Slow Down

Psychologists have become part of the fabric of modern sports. As an example, one baseball manager discussed getting a player involved in a tense situation to relax by encouraging him to slow the heart rate; slow the thinking process; just slow it down. Instead of rushing, take a second, take a breath, and assess what is going on around you.

Jimmy Buffett, in his song in the aftermath of Hurricane Katrina, captured it best, "Breathe in, Breathe Out, Move On"[20]. A fine lesson to slow down a bit and follow the widely adopted STAR program – Stop Think Act Review[21].

Media relations professionals teach that you should hang up the phone from a media call before answering the reporters' questions. Take five minutes to think through the answer and then call back. Slowing down allows you to think through a proposal or a response before giving an answer that might ultimately win or lose many jobs. Slow down, think like a professional, and then move on.

Coming in Second
With winning as the ultimate goal, there are no Silver Medals in economic development. Pro golfer Walter Hagen famously declared, "No one remembers who came in second." But there are often key lessons to learn from the losing position if you are willing and paying attention. The best responses to coming in "second" are:

---

20 Music by Matt Betton and Jimmy Buffett, "*Breathe In, Breathe Out, Move On*", RCA, October 2006

21 Star was developed by DDI, Development Dimensions, International, Inc. in 1974, https://www.ddiworld.com/about/history. Was shared with Ameren, Missouri's Callaway Nuclear Power Plant, https://www.ameren.com/-/media/corporate-site/files/careers/star-model-behavioral-interview.pdf?la=en&hash=3979D26080AB4FDA11609DBB805CEFFD5775F14A. This was borrowed by International Space Station (ISS) Space Flight Resource Management SFRM). See website   https://ntrs.nasa.gov/archive/nasa/casi.ntrs.nasa.gov/20080041534. pdf for the article by Evelyn Baldwin, Integrating Space Flight Resource Management Skills Into Technical Lessons For International Space Station Flight Controller Training, 2008. Subsequently STAR moved into healthcare, education, and business.

- Express your disappointment with class and dignity.
- Compliment the company on their choice and wish them well.
- Listen to what they liked about your community, but also why the other community fits their needs better.
- Always leave the door open – never, ever burn a bridge with the company or site consultant – you may want to cross it again. Amazon HQ2 is a great example.
- Keep in touch – it will not usually reverse the decision, but that is not the point. Let them know you want to be considered in the future.
- Remember, economic development is a long-term business and process. Seeds take time, patience, and work to germinate.
- Brief your staff and leadership team while being mindful of what the confidentiality agreement allows. Have a session to discuss what we need to work on for the next project visit. If you can learn why you lost or deciding factors, communicate the message to your team with an action plan to correct any problems.
- Look in the mirror – did you do everything you could to win the project? If so, then go get a good night's sleep.
- Move on to the next project to grow or expand jobs in your community with hard-earned lessons for application from the ones that got away.

It is important to recognize those times when you should not expend your resources competing for a particular project. If your community just does not have the necessary match with the prospect's resource needs or fit with their objectives, then do not waste your limited resources. From personal experience, I had to call my boss, the governor, on a couple of occasions and basically say, "we cannot win this project." If you find yourself in that situation, think it through, get your facts, make the case, and then move on to the next job creation opportunity.

CHAPTER 4
HIGH DEFINITION COMMUNITY

Bedford was established more than a hundred and fifty years ago as a mid-west settlement that blossomed as the railroad and ensuing settlers discovered a thriving community. The city continued to grow, relying on agriculture and manufacturing as their main sources of employment until the 1970s when Bedford began to see jobs relocated offshore because of lower wages.

Thus, began a clinical look at Bedford and how the community could sustain itself in an evolving economy. The EDA's first economic development 'professional' backed into the job having served for five years as the chamber's membership director.

Those initial years were a learning process for everyone. As the organization grew it became apparent a more seasoned team was needed. David was recruited and immediately began filling the open slots with quality, diverse professionals. Things began to turn around for the organization and Bedford.

The local government officials began to understand the role they played in successful job creation and Bedford became one of the state's more attractive mid-sized cities with a pride in the community that had not fully existed in decades. Nevertheless, they had not won a major project in several years' and the community's leadership team was becoming a bit antsy.

Now, Project Penguin would test a lot of work that had been done to create infrastructure, improve local education, and build a quality of life that people from all over raved about. But now the test also included economic recovery from the pandemic and stretched everyone's resources in the process – good thing they were all working together.

There are many "good" communities across America competing for relatively few attraction and retention projects each year. Most community leaders are like those from Lake Wobegon who tout that all our kids are above average, and life is wonderful. The fact is America is blessed with many "good" communities but the objective in successful economic development is to stand out from the rest of the "good" areas – to become a **high definition community** that stays in the game throughout the elimination rounds.

For anyone who has bought a new television lately, it is all about advanced technology and high definition. Ultra HDTVs cost more and so do high definition communities. In addition to a skilled workforce pipeline, and available product, companies are looking for communities who take pride in their cities. People searching for a suitable site know a community's pride translates directly into their businesses should they make your community their final choice. There are no size or resource requirements per se for a high definition community, but one **ready for economic development done right** with the commitment and resources[22] in place to achieve the community's objectives.

---

22 Do not forget allies as a source for resources. They win when you win and will want to help.

Every community should have a living, breathing strategic economic development plan – living, breathing translates into getting meaningful value through implementing actions. The emphasis is on execution rather than fluff.

Some experts recommend just a one-page business plan rather than a weighty document with too little beef and a lot of bun, an advertising image embraced in the 1984 Wendy's Hamburger chain ad slogan. Actress Clara Peller buys a burger with a massive bun. The small patty prompts Peller to angrily exclaim, "Where's the Beef?"[23] (Unfortunately, some companies and site consultants might think or even say the same thing following a community's presentation.)

Planning is important as long as it is appropriately simple, focused, and honest with the main emphasis on execution.[24] Often, communities try too hard to be all things when it is much better to have accomplished a few things at 100% rather than have a laundry list that looks and sounds good but is never fully achieved.

It's all about focus and execution. Today's successful football coaches approach the game with a strategic plan in place and the know-how, focus, and resources to implement the plan. In University of Alabama Coach Nick Saban's case, he refers to it as the **Process**[25]. The Process is a way of breaking down a difficult situation into manageable steps and the

---

23 The "Where's the Beef?" advertising campaign for Wendy's fast food restaurant was created by the Dancer Fitzgerald Sample advertising agency.

24 What does execution require? Make a Decision on your goal then Identify Actions to be taken:
- Agree on Work Assignments: W^3 and How – [W^3 = Who, What, & When]
- Make Clear Task Assignments
- Structure Action in Achievable Chunks
- Identify Performance Measures

25 Constant Renewal, 2019 Newsletter, www.constantrenewal.com

same approach can apply to establishing a high definition community.

The One Thing in Life

In the movie *City Slickers*[26], Curly (Jack Palance) kept telling Billy Crystal about discovering the "...one thing in life." Crystal keeps pestering Curly for the answer and he finally says that the one thing in life is different for everyone. "You have to discover it for yourself." So, it is with the economic development process for your team and community. Every economic developer should have a process that fits her or his organization and community personality. It can begin with some basic questions about the current situation:

- Where are we now as a community and/or economic development organization? This requires an honest analysis and a **realistic** view. One process for the community or region includes an economic development vitality index[27] that establishes a benchmark on six key pillars from which communities can begin implementing a plan. The community vitality index essentially provides the community with a score, similar to a personal credit score, based on key indicators and becomes a guidepost for community improvement.

---

26 *City Slickers*, Castlerock Entertainment, Ron Underwood Director, released 1991

27 Vitality indexes are used to measure economic and social wellbeing. They have been crafted by states, e.g., Georgia and by other organizations, e.g., the Brookings Institute. The above vitality index was developed and calculated specifically for economic development purposes. Therefore most of the pillars are different.

1. Population,
2. Education/Workforce,
3. Leadership,
4. Charm Factor,
5. Infrastructure, and
6. Site Selection Pluses and Minuses

- Based on the community vitality score, where do we want to be in one year, three years or five years? In other words, what is the vision your community should embrace? As the Bible says in Proverbs (29.18), "Without vision, the people perish." A blind person asked St. Anthony "Can there be anything worse than losing your eyesight?" St. Anthony replied, "Yes, losing your vision."[28]

- Planning should move to reality by developing an Action Plan[29]. Walter Isaacson, former president of *The Aspen Institute,* said on a CBS Sunday Morning program, "Vision without execution is simply hallucination."[30]

- How do we get there from here and what is the Process necessary to navigate the journey? In *"Butch Cassidy and the Sundance Kid,"[31]* an exchange highlights the need for clear direction. Sundance says to Butch: "Which way?" To which Butch casually replies, "It doesn't matter. I don't know where we've been, and I've just been there."

---

28 *What Grandpa John Says About Life,* John Kalenberg, Xlibris Corporation, 2012

29 The purpose of planning is to take action. The plan enables the organization to maximize the impact of its resources on achieving its priorities. An action plan includes the goal, what specifically will be done, who is responsible, what resources (including human) they have, how results will be measured, and a timeline for completion.

30 Walter Isaacson, CBS Morning News, October 12, 2014. The quote has frequently been attributed to Thomas Edison and Henry Ford.

31 *"Butch Cassidy and the Sundance Kid"*, George Roy Hill Director, 20th Century Fox, September 23, 1969

- How do we measure progress along the way? What are the benchmarks necessary to establish a workable accountability system? Who has ownership of the Process?
- Can we get some early wins to give the community team a sense of achievement? Do not try to accomplish everything in the plan at first – pick some low-hanging fruit and score some wins recognizing that full accomplishment takes time.
- How disruptive do we have to be to achieve the goals? What is a needed disruptive process for both the professional economic developer and the community?

Through the Eyes of the Decision-Maker

Communities and economic development organizations must also look at their location through the eyes of the project decision-maker or the expanding local existing company who may be asking the key question: "Where does your community stand with regard to these factors important in my decision?"

- Access to my markets
- Access to the talent necessary to be successful and profitable today and tomorrow
- Access to supply-chain resources – the five most important supply chain factors:
    - Cost
    - Speed – getting the product to the client on time
    - Quality of service
    - Reliability
    - Consistency
- Access to available sites/buildings/space
- Access to capital
- Both the real and perceived impact of government regulations on my business
- As key personnel relocate to the community, what quality of life will they experience? An even better question: Is it about

the same or worse than their current location? In many searches, these "soft" issues become major decision points.

• And, what is the situation with K-12 education for my relocated personnel and their families? Is it better, about the same, or worse than their current location? This may also be a factor.

These factors should be researched and addressed even before there is an active project, especially from a targeted marketing and community planning standpoint.

Where Do We Want to Go? What Do We Want to Be?

Strategic Economic Development Planning is a process most communities employ at one time or another, often with less than satisfactory results. Initiating a strategic plan is not usually the issue – the difficulty comes with implementation of a living, breathing plan. Too often, the nicely bound 98-page manual sits in a bookcase after some government or agency forked over $40,000 and the community becomes jaded by the lack of progress with a flawed process.[32]

---

32 We have two thoughts to share with you about strategic planning:
1. To determine if your Strategic Plan is little more than wishful thinking or has a chance of success just look at the Table of Contents. Are Target Markets mentioned? Does it include an Action Plan of what to do now and in the near future? In order to work effectively and efficiently toward goals you need to know which industrial targets, allies, and locals you intend to target with your plan's efforts. Your SWOT only has meaning when you match what the firms and people you are interacting with want and need. You can't do everything. Why not focus what you intend to do and your resources on the wants and needs of the people and organizations you plan to influence? This is what is needed to win, so organize your resources and what people are working on accordingly.
2. When things are changing like now, the rules for strategy success also change. This is good for any economic development organization that can adapt its strategy to meet the new marketplace conditions. Of course, this means you need to be paying attention to your existing business and anyone else you are trying to influence. Which new requirements will be easier

It is important for the community to engage in a process that identifies both the community strengths and weaknesses but also offers a pathway to accomplish objectives, preferably in manageable chunks. Additionally, do not forget different target markets may have different views of your SWOT. What is a weakness to one target industry may be a strength to another.

Many organizations employ some version of a SWOT Analysis Process: Strengths, Weaknesses, Opportunities, and Threats. In its simplest form a SWOT analysis looks at leveraging capabilities, assets, and resources to accomplish your goals vs. minimizing or mitigating risks and threats.[33]

- **Strengths** - What do you do well? What unique resources can be drawn upon and how can your community leverage its strengths for good? Which customers are the best match for our strengths now? How can we improve to be a better match for potential customers in the near term? Longer-term?
- **Weaknesses** – What is their impact on the ability to reach community goals? When addressing can they be minimized or eliminated? Whose help is needed to tackle the weaknesses?
- **Opportunities** – What opportunities are open now or on the near horizon and how can strengths be turned into opportunities for quality job growth? Which opportunities

---

for your community to provide? Which messages need to be changed? Amplified? Smaller communities can move faster than large ones. Take advantage of this opportunity.

33 Many use OTSW – beginning with Opportunities and Threats will focus an organization's efforts on the Strengths and Weaknesses which matter to the target customers, both in the short and long-term. Pay particular attention to your allies - their capabilities are important to the ability to address and, hopefully, reach community goals..

match our present capabilities best? What is the long-term vision focused on? How will the decisions made in the short-term improve our ability to achieve long-term goals?

- **Threats** – What threats and emerging issues could harm growth efforts and impact implementation of the community's strategic growth plan?

It is important for a community and an economic development organization to focus on all of the SWOT elements, especially in the most positive manner possible. In reality, community leaders and stakeholders really do not want to hear negatives, even though it is a necessary step toward becoming a high definition community. Every weakness and threat can be couched in terms that offer hope and provide a successful pathway to impact the community's competitiveness for expansion, attraction, and home-grown jobs.

Strengths describe the positive factors in a community. From an economic development standpoint, anything that is likely to provide an edge over the competition is a strength. Sometimes, strengths and weaknesses are inextricably linked. Suppose your community has great airport sites for the aerospace industry but the region is lacking the talent pipeline necessary to staff an advanced aerospace manufacturing or assembly operation. Then both the strengths and weaknesses need to be factored into effective target marketing to the aerospace sector while the labor weakness needs to become part of your community's action items to address and, hopefully, solve.

What are their impacts on the ability to reach community goals? When addressing, can they be minimized or eliminated? Whose help is needed to tackle the weaknesses? Throughout the SWOT or Vitality Index Process, it is important to focus on solutions or mitigating actions for the weaknesses. What will mitigate a weakness given who you are trying to influence and what is the process necessary to turn it to a strength or, at least, neutralize it?

Opportunities reflect the potential of a community. An effective SWOT Analysis is interrelated or intertwined. Identification of strengths and weaknesses will probably present new opportunities, especially as weaknesses are improved or eliminated. For instance, as a community attracts enhanced broadband and high technology capability, new opportunities emerge to market this gained strength to certain industries and technology clusters which were not targets.

Changes in government regulations may reduce previous barriers to a whole new industry sector. Coupling strengths with improved or eliminated weaknesses and applying them to an effective economic development strategy is a prime objective of the SWOT process. New targeted market doors should also be identified and opened.

Threats come in all shapes and sizes and can be either external or internal. Threats are anything that can adversely affect a community, such as inflation, business costs, punitive legislation or regulations, elections, leadership changes, or an aggressive competitor in the region. All those threats plus the major impact of the global pandemic reinforce the importance of facing them as a High Definition Community.

The DNA or Vitality Index

Another way to examine a community is to conduct an economic development **DNA** which is an oft-used medical term for a community economic development vitality index. A medical DNA, or deoxyribonucleic acid, is a look inside the unique body to define who you are – helps determine what you look like and other personal traits. An economic development DNA is a process that looks inside each community to define its unique characteristics and provide steps to improve its economic competitiveness.

A Vitality Index Process or an economic development DNA should have continuous monitoring, actions, accountability, and revisions for effectiveness. Whatever the process is called, it must be organized and structured so community leaders, and constituents, feel comfortable coming together to take action and generate solutions to common problems.

The Process should allow the community to get rid of all the clutter, the "stupid stuff" that impedes progress. Forrest Gump[34] famously said, "Stupid is as stupid does." In words attributed to John Wayne, "Life's hard. It's even harder when you do stupid things."

Stephen Covey cautions that the common flaw in ambitious people (in this case ambitious plans) is to set so many goals that you cannot achieve any of them.[35] An organized Process requires prioritization, which forces surrendering the clutter and the "stupid stuff," thereby allowing a workable pathway to implementation.

The Wake-up Call

A Process requires an owner. One who wakes up every morning thinking about the issues identified through an honest, candid assessment. Otherwise, the chances of meaningful actions are slim and the effort will eventually fall into the abyss of everyday activity or rest neatly on a bookshelf.

The key to a high definition community is to concentrate on what actually causes success for a city, county, or state. Remember "A good process produces good results."

Many have concluded that cities and communities are the last bastion of effectively addressing the economic, social, and environmental challenges within our states and country. In our opinions, cities and communities are likely to handle these challenges in a way that is more efficient, more effective, and more democratic than Washington, D.C.

---

34 *Forrest Gump*, Director Robert Lee Zemeckis, 1994, U.S.A.

35 Stephen Covey, *The 7 Habits of Effective People*, Habit 3, First Things First, Simon & Schuster, 1989.

Emphasis on economic growth should begin in the communities across the country – in America's heartland. In many rural communities the quality of life is declining. Lack of steady paychecks from the pandemic and other factors have affected the ability of many to keep their house payments current so the resulting economic decline ripples throughout the community.

Many workers now commute long distances to work just to have a paycheck. Violence has increased partially because of the long time away from home leaves many youth unsupervised and restless. Substance abuse is rampant in many declining areas and some, once vibrant communities, have turned into stagnant places.

The good news is that we may be in a time where large, medium, and small cities have the potential to emerge from decades of population decline, pandemic recovery, economic stagnation, and job loss into striving communities that contribute to thriving states. Some have attacked the issues directly as Nashville did by tearing down walls and convincing people that they can make a difference. Revivals in motivated cities are growing and sustaining jobs for local residents, generating tax revenues for local services/ schools, and creating a sense of community pride.

One can study The Tupelo Model,[36] based on the community's efforts in Tupelo, Mississippi, to reinvent itself as a thriving economic center. A visit now to that northeastern Mississippi city of 40,000 displays the job creation fruits that took more than 30 years to fully incubate. Several major think tanks have studied many of the precepts of the model founded on local citizens addressing local problems, treating each person as a partner resource, employing the old adage of teaching people to fish, tearing down the walls that often separate organizations and government entities, and building a community that honors leadership principles across all sectors.

---

36 www.cdfms.org

The Ford Institute's approach,[37] in line with the Tupelo Model, builds a base of human, leadership, organizational, and community "capital" **before** depending on recruiting and attracting new companies as the foundation of job creation. While this is not always the popular approach, it is certainly the most successful because it forces a community to attack key competitive issues first and then embark on a well-thought-out, targeted attraction strategy.

The fact that success came in rural Mississippi underscores the adage that "demographics do not always determine destiny." It **is** hard work and a long process becoming a high definition community but, as with Nashville, Tupelo, and many communities across the country, the results are worth it.

Disruption Includes Rethinking

Disruptive economic development almost always includes rethinking challenges, vision, strategies, and measuring outcomes. Rethinking as a part of the process encourages redefining what is around you – the assets, liabilities, opportunities, and challenges. Rethinking can also debunk some long-held myths about the community and what is taken for granted. Disrupters examine the holistic community to see where opportunities lie for positive change. Thus, rethinking creates new options for economic and job growth.

The debate continues about what is community and what is economic development. **Community development comes before economic development, or at least it should**. Getting the community primed for "economic development" seems a natural step before initiating a robust new company recruiting process. The

---

37   FordInstituteWorkingTogether_v10.pdf Ford Institute for Community Building, Community Vitality, Vol. XII/Issue 1, Spring 2012, Joyce Akse; https://www.tfff.org/what-we-do/vital-rural-communities/ford-institute-community-building/community-building-approach

old adage on the golf course of "getting the bet right" before the first shot seems appropriate.

In the mid-twentieth century there was a program popular with rural communities – the Prepared Cities Program[38]. If you met certain criteria, your community could be designated as a prepared city for economic growth. While the program does not exist today, it is a sound concept.

Quite simply, "prepared" indicated on paper that a community had done the necessary due diligence to be competitive for job creation. The times were much different from today and the lack of results not as dramatically visible. Today in many rural communities and with the growing migration to the urban areas, being prepared for economic success truly impacts scores of citizens and often determines a community's economic destiny.

However, being a truly prepared community is a hard, continuous process that requires constant review, action, and inclusion. Follow the same formula for your planning efforts. Don't wait for a year to re-visit your strategy. Your customers and competitors are not on your timeline. They can change their decision criteria and/ or approach at any time. Pay attention to the marketplace and the signals being sent. That is where you will win or lose.

---

38 A description of the program is located here: *Intergovernmental Perspective* magazine, Winter, 1981, Page 18, available at https://books.google.com/books

CHAPTER 5

OPERATING ON
EIGHT CYLINDERS –
A WELL-OILED MACHINE

Not long after he arrived in Bedford, David began looking at the staff and volunteer leadership. He had visited several well-run economic development organizations and all said that putting together a professional staff with good chemistry and diverse skills would pay huge dividends. Again, they likened it to sports. The coach needed a strong cadre of assistant coaches that he/she could rely on and trust to bring about the needed results.

Betsy moved to the EDA from the planning department and Adrienne was recruited from the local electric utility. With the addition of Craig, they had a staff that could finally focus efforts on all the important job creation fronts.

As the EDA gained more experience, one of the strongest business leaders stepped up to help organize the first board of directors. Mike Reid's family had been in Bedford for three generations and he had inherited the family's construction company. The family had seen the ups and downs of wars, recessions, booms, and busts. Mike majored in business at the state university and always knew he would come home to Bedford to continue the family business.

He once had a fleeting thought about running for the state legislature but, at the last minute, decided he could have a greater impact at home, focused on Bedford and his young family. The community was evolving and wrong decisions could impact the city they loved and it was "home."

Now, Mike had the opportunity to help craft a strong economic development agency that could contribute to economic stability for his family and neighbors. But, just as the construction business was rough-and-tumble, he quickly learned that economic development competition and local egos were even more brutal.

With several other key local leaders Mike put together a strong inaugural EDA board of directors. One of their first acts was to travel to a city in the South that was comparable in size and demographics but had fought and won some of the same battles Bedford now experienced. The meetings and tours confirmed that the southern counterpart had established itself as a leading growth and innovation hub – Mike and his team wanted to learn from both their mistakes and good decisions so Bedford could replicate the right steps and try to avoid as many wrong moves as possible.

Looking back on the fam trip, everyone realized it opened eyes that were blind, or at least not focused, and helped guide some key decisions in setting up a strong EDA and charting goals and a strong foundation for the community. Little did they know a decade ago that their decisions would shape the professional EDA but also provide the nucleus for tackling one of the country's greatest economic challenges and one that hit Bedford especially hard.

I t's always disconcerting when an expensive automobile is only operating on five or six cylinders when it should be grooving on all eight. In an orchestra, everyone plays a different part to make beautiful music. As you enter the concert hall and hear the orchestra members getting ready for the performance, tuning their instruments with a sound that is at best incoherent and undistinguishable, you might wonder about the quality of the performers. However, when the maestro arrives and lifts the baton to begin the concerto, all doubts are erased about the talents so many seemingly different players now exhibit. Together, in harmony, the most beautiful music fills the hall.

So it is with a finely-tuned economic development team. Each community participant plays their role in partnership with the others, recognizing that together they can present beautiful music through a truly synchronized EDO and community. Each player must know his/her role and allow others to do theirs as well. This truism impacts the internal staff and also radiates throughout the community structure.

More and more economic development organizations employ various leadership formulas to encourage both staff and volunteers. John Osborne, who heads the Lubbock, Texas Economic Development Alliance swears by a set of non-negotiable Core Values. He holds both his staff and volunteer leaders to the essential principles outlined on one sheet of paper.

With appreciation to John for sharing Lubbock's Core Values which can be used or adapted for any economic development organization:

- **Attitude is Everything** – A positive attitude projects internally and externally. A positive attitude is the key to encouraging, acknowledging, and appreciating the work of others.
- **Be Trustworthy** – Always do the right things, even when no one is looking. Always respect those in our community; remembering our word is our bond.
- **Communicate** – Take a proactive approach to ensure that all levels of the community are informed in a professional and respectful manner. Express your ideas clearly

when speaking and actively listen. Honor commitments to confidentiality.

- **Family First** – Perform at the same levels at home as you do at work. Excellence at home equals excellence at work.
- **Foster Success** – Cultivate and encourage a forward-thinking environment that embraces creativity and diversity, providing support and resources that nurture each individual's unique skills. Empower and trust in others and strive for excellence. All achievements big or small should be recognized
- **Serve Others** – *Uncompromising* commitment to our community and to each other.
- **Work in Wisdom** – Work hard, work smart, have fun, produce while striving to achieve goals, and make good things happen. Be open and receptive to new ideas and guidance in dealings within the community and be willing to share your experiences and knowledge to produce and reach a successful result. Be a humble teacher; be a willing learner. Remember: there is no limit to what can be accomplished as long as you don't care who gets the credit.

Lubbock, Texas Economic Development Alliance[39]

Various Models

Across the United States, about five thousand economic development organizations operate under one of several organizational models.

The **private agency** derives financial support from businesses, industries, and chambers of commerce and does not accept government funding. Its board and stakeholders are from the private sector and, good or bad, has an arms-length relationship with

---

39 https://lubbockeda.org/

government entities. The private model can also maintain project and issue confidentiality[40] more easily than other models.

Some job creation agencies are totally **government-funded**, and staff members are city/county/state employees. The local mayor/council/commission usually provides policy direction/oversight and the organization has a more direct connection to government functions and resources. As a downside, it can be tough maintaining project confidentiality, especially in a state with strong "sunshine" laws.

The hybrid of the private and government structures is a **public-private** organization with funding coming from both sectors and policy direction from a diverse public-private board. The obvious advantage of this structure is the ability to solicit funding from both sides of the aisle and the disadvantages range from confidentiality challenges to differences in policy from public and private stakeholders.

With any model, the step-by-step process to establish or re-engineer a solid organization is essentially the same:

- Find good comparable, successful organizations and learn what they have done right/wrong. Most organizations are willing to share their experiences knowing that, one day, they may need reciprocal counsel.
- Craft a mission statement coupled with a set of core values that clearly states the purpose of the organization. (This will affect the accountability aspect of the organization.) Additionally, draft a set of by-laws that are workable for your community, stakeholders, and organization.

---

40 Confidentiality when dealing with a competitive project is one of the most sacred principles in economic development. Almost every site consultant or company decision-maker requires that a project be kept confidential to protect the selection process. In fact, cases exist where communities have been eliminated from the selection process because they violated the confidentiality agreement.

- With the usual exception of a totally public organization, establish a steering/executive committee of community leaders who are willing to become actively involved in the effort. The by-laws and core values should set parameters for both an executive committee and board of directors. Be sure the organization is protected from political or powerful manipulation.
- Staff the agency with diverse professionals. Diversity in gender, race, and thought/communication approaches can enhance the effectiveness of an organization. Remember the old adage, "You are only as good as your weakest link."
- Determine an appropriate funding level that will accomplish the job creation mission based on the Goldilocks model: Not too hot, not too cold, but just right!
- Annually revisit your organizational structure, core values, and team capabilities – not easy but necessary to determine if resources are being deployed in the best manner to accomplish the stated goals – some organizations call it zero-based budgeting or planning.
- Determine funding sources to meet the community's job creation goals and develop a plan to secure the necessary resources. Remember your allies can help.
- Sell the organization and its mission to the targeted stakeholders (funders) based on a strong return on investment.

The Mother's Milk of Economic Development

Harvard Business School's Michael Porter says that satisfied investors must understand the shared value they have in the community. He defines shared value as "...policies and operating practices that enhance the competitiveness of a company while simultaneously advancing the economic and social conditions in the communities in which it operates...shared value is not social responsibility, philanthropy, or even sustainability, but a new way to achieve economic success."[41] Porter continues that "A business needs a successful community, not only to create public assets and a supportive environment. A community needs *successful businesses to provide jobs and wealth creation opportunities for its citizens.*"[42] (Italics added)

Remember the abbreviated definition of economic development: the process of creating new wealth. Therefore, an economic development organization's mission is to be the instrument that helps a community "...achieve economic success."

Another popular term related to funding an organization is establishing the "value proposition" for economic development as the agency tasked to grow jobs. Stakeholders want to know what they are getting for their money and need to be reminded often. Fostering and sustaining investment partners is almost a daily effort and is easy if you remember your successful use of their funds/resources encourages them to give you more.

Many organizations personally visit their stakeholders quarterly or semi-annually to strengthen the lines of communication and feedback. Also, most agencies hold monthly, bi-monthly, or at least quarterly meetings for stakeholders to keep them informed as a group, often having an outside speaker discuss a topic that directly affects economic development success in the community.

The opportunities for face-to-face interaction should be supplemented by periodic communication to stakeholders outlining the current job creation efforts and outcome measures of their agency. (Remember, it is **their** agency!)

In the Confidential "Know"

Stakeholders want to be in the "confidential know." With various investor levels, this presents unique challenges because those giving the most expect to know the most. Or in reality, those giving

---

41 Michael Porter and Mark Kramer, "*Creating Shared Value,*" Harvard Business Review, January 2011, page 4.

42 Ibid, Page 7.

anything want to know the most! Successful organizations communicate investor benefits from the beginning so that each stakeholder level is aware of the ingredients or perks of their particular investment package. It also presents unique challenges with project confidentiality – how much can you discuss without violating both the spirit and letter of project confidentiality agreements. Identifying active projects presents enormous risks to the integrity of the process and may call into question the organization's favoritism if revealed to a select few. But the disclosure of active projects is the one thing that investors want to know so dealing with that issue from the beginning can save a lot of grief. Set a policy that balances investor "wants" with project confidentiality.

With airline Frequent Flyer programs, there is a big difference between Silver and Platinum members. The perks are there for both but at much different levels. The challenge for organizations is to craft a process so that *all* members/stakeholders believe they are getting value for their investment. Make the benefits clear upfront but continue to emphasize the overall benefit their investment is making to the growth of the community – and, ultimately to their individual business or firm.

Managing the various levels of investors is a key role for the economic development staff. In today's business economy, investors want value in the product (and the EDA is a product!).

Today's investors tend to be more cautious and less willing to make a long-term commitment. And, it's no longer automatic that existing stakeholders will renew without receiving attention and realizing tangible results for their investment. With today's countless competitive support opportunities, companies are scrutinizing investments in non-profit organizations more closely than ever. And, the pandemic negative impact on business revenue has affected the funding levels for many community organizations including government-funded or supported economic development agencies.

The organization should connect at a deep level to energize investors. There should be no surprise with an investor's attitude toward the EDA. If there is, then the staff and officers have not been doing their jobs communicating and interacting with the investor base.

The Campaign

Before initiating a funding campaign, an organization should objectively evaluate:

- The EDA's image in the community – positive, negative, professional, results-oriented?
- How its case for funding will be viewed by potential investors – is there a strong reason to invest? Has the "value proposition" been seeded?
- Availability of quality campaign leaders – people give to people they know and respect.
- Are these the right target investors? Do they have the capacity to contribute at a reasonable level?
- Is the agency board of directors firmly supportive and invested? Board members should be enthusiastic, committed, and capable of providing seed capital and continuing support.
- What are the community and economic development organizations' realistic job creation goals? Are we willing to be held accountable to these goals?
- What new jobs do you count? There is an old economic development adage: "Shoot at everything that flies, count everything that falls." In today's business-savvy world of investors, that adage won't cut it. Plus, it's just an incorrect strategy. Each organization must be able to defend every new job it counts toward the annual goal based on realistic and acceptable criteria. And, the agency should certainly

not be shooting at everything that flies – it needs a targeted, well-thought-out strategy.

Your allies are just as important. They have objectives to achieve and many are after the same results as your organization. Be sure you help them achieve their objectives. They will help you achieve yours.

Metrics: In the end, investors and elected officials will always expect accountability on jobs created. It is the one goal that cannot be dismissed or minimized. The creation of new jobs, either through expansion, attraction, or innovation, can be coupled with other important metrics but cannot mitigate the importance of job and new wealth creation.

Reports to investors and elected officials should also focus on the increase in per capita income for the community/county; the capital investment from expanding and recruited companies; and the impact of the numbers from the "ripple effect" of direct, induced, and indirect job creation.[43]

It is important to paint a complete picture of the agency's accomplishments and involvement in the job creation process. Reports should remain consistent in methodology so stakeholders can track progress. Accountability and return on investment are critical to stakeholder confidence and buy-in.

It is also important to remind the professional economic developer, the elected official, and the stakeholder involved in the process that economic development is **not** a consumption item. Successful job creation comes as seeds are planted, watered,

---

43 Direct economic impact results from wages and spending at primary industries. Indirect economic impact results from the primary industries' direct spending at secondary companies i.e. industry suppliers. Induced economic impact results from spending in the local grocery stores, retail establishments, and restaurants by employees of the primary industry, the suppliers, and direct service firms.

cultivated, and harvested which takes time. No one can relate to this better than the farmers across America because they will testify that growing crops to harvest is very hard work.

Anthropologists say the Agricultural Revolution began about 10,000 years ago. Man began to plant and harvest crops which allowed the establishment of towns and societies. That principle of abundance is illustrated throughout Holy Scriptures, especially "We reap as we sow. If we sow abundantly, we will reap in abundance; if we sow sparingly, we will reap sparingly." Our role is to sow generously and work through the process to see what our efforts reap. And, once the harvest is complete, the ground plowed and the seeds planted for the next crop season, the process begins all over again – the economic development circle of life.

CHAPTER 6

HIGH ACHIEVING COMMUNITIES REQUIRE UNCONVENTIONAL LEADERSHIP

"Look, I don't really know where we should take this
bus. But I know this much: If we get the right people
on the bus, the right people in the right seats, and the
wrong people off the bus, then we'll figure out how to
take it someplace great."
Jim Collins, Good to Great

Looking back over his five years in Bedford, David realized the key
to a quality economic development agency was the fresh volunteer
leadership that helped mold and undergird the organization.

One of the city's native sons taught leadership at the state's
major land grant university and he gladly contributed his time to
school the young team on the kind of leaders and process necessary
to grow both the agency and the community. He also cautioned
them about patience. Positive changes take time, resources, and
effort.

The active stakeholders came from the usual suspects but also some surprising corners. Rick Page, a local accountant, emerged as one of the EDA's go-getters and strategic thinkers. The downtown Methodist pastor, Charles Barnes, brought a perspective that helped the board look at all sectors of the community. And a retired plant manager from the state's capital city brought a passion for management expertise and tapping into the retired community for entrepreneur mentors. An accomplished author, Cheryl Lee, used her international experiences to help the local team prepare for international prospects and guests.

The first couple of years ended up being a key to the EDA's successful future. A diverse and active board gave overall direction to the staff but allowed them the freedom to do their jobs. And when it was showtime, they assembled a great leadership team to present their growing community to the world or just the company operating down the street.

In fact, David took the EDA director's job in part because of the leadership on the board and throughout the community.

Now the "show time" revolved around Project Penguin, but also the presentation in a week to the City Council on a Bedford Pandemic Recovery Plan. Project Penguin was the opportunity for a home run. Singles and doubles are good but it sure was nice to get a chance for the long ball – especially when the nation's economy was teetering on a recession. Therefore, the pandemic recovery plan was very important too!

A research report by The Cousins Research Group (a division of the Kettering Foundation) and written by Kettering Foundation president David Mathews makes the case for "leaderfulness" if communities want to become high achievers.[44] The report discusses the ability to change and adapt when faced with challenges recognizing

---

44 David Matthews, *Leaders or Leaderfulness: Lessons from High-Achieving Communities*, https://www.kettering.org/catalog/product/leaders-or-leaderfulness

that solutions must come from every sector in the community. As John Gardner put it in the report, "communities need initiative takers from every part of the community and in every facet of community life."[45]

Conventional leadership often celebrates the accomplishments of one person and his/her "leadership" skills. In other words, the "go-to" person. But, throughout sports history, the real championship "teams" come from a unique chemistry that melds diverse skills and personalities into a fully charged dream automobile hitting on all cylinders. Unconventional leadership celebrates the accomplishments of an entire community. As the old adage says, one person does not win competitive job creation projects, it takes an entire community.

Hundreds of books and thousands of articles have been written on leadership, especially the individual leadership that gets the most publicity. Jesus Christ. Winston Churchill. Franklin Roosevelt. Mother Teresa. Douglas McArthur. Stephen Covey. Nelson Mandela. Harry Truman.

But the real need in economic development is communities of "leaderfulness" - recognizing that a community will not become a striving, high definition community unless every facet of the community is brought into the process. Yes, there must be leaders who influence others to action. P.G. Northouse defines leadership as "a process whereby individuals influence *groups* of individuals to achieve shared goals."[46] Clearly, leaders must be able to inspire people to strongly desire and believe in what the leader, the organization, and the cause stands for. Quite often, there is the nagging, selfish question, "what's in it for me?" Leaders must be able to make a compelling case for collective impact or the natural tendency will be to stay satisfied with the status quo.

---

45 John Gardner, *"Leadership Papers/11: The Changing Nature of Leadership"* (Washington, DC: The Independent Sector, 1988), 8. Gardner discusses the need to devolve responsibility for decision making among many people at the grassroots level.

46 Northouse, P.G. (2010). *Leadership: Theory and Practice* (5th ed). Thousand Oaks, CA: SAGE Publications, page 2

Under the concept of "leaderfulness," the more people brought into the equation, the easier it becomes to generate action and movement and thus acceptance by the constituency. Rare are the days when communities can grow and become great by securing just the support of top community leadership. Striving communities embrace a big tent approach.

By its very nature, economic development involves change. With new jobs and resulting increased wealth, a community has a strong opportunity to change for the good. In the reverse, stagnant communities see jobs decline and incomes diminish. Change, either way, is inevitable, you cannot stay where you are. Like all human institutions, you are growing or dying.

In Tom Peters' book, *Thriving on Chaos*[47], he states "...the most obvious benefit of unsettled times is the unique opportunity they afford to create rapid change. For those of vision, chaos can facilitate innovation." In an unsettled community undergoing change, individuals with vision and positive attitudes - those willing to embrace change - can help move the community in the desired direction.

For example, if the community is targeting aerospace and aviation projects, but the talent pipeline cannot support an aerospace project's job criteria, then the decision becomes – accept the status quo mediocrity, or improve the talent pipeline to coincide with targeted industry sectors. The change agent economic developer will work within his/her leadership team and the education community to move into a more competitive situation. The successful economic developer cannot sit back and accept the status quo. Leadership guru John Maxwell says, "The pessimist complains about the wind. The optimist expects it to change. The leader adjusts the sails."[48] This is the essence of disruptive economic development – using your leadership position to initiate positive changes in a community's competitive status.

47 Tom Peters, *Thriving on Chaos: A Handbook of Management Revolution*, Alfred A. Knopf, Inc. 1987.

48 John Maxwell Minute, March 23, 2012

Perhaps the most overlooked leadership challenge is self. Leadership expert Dee Hock wrote that "It is management of the self that should occupy 50% of our time and the best of our ability. And when we do that the ethical, moral, and spiritual elements of management are inescapable. The best gift you can give those you lead is a healthy, energized, and focused self."[49]

Part of the focus on self is the acceptance and recognition of good, honest feedback from others and to others, especially those you depend on at home and in the workplace. Remember, most everyone you meet has no idea what economic development is, does, or how you perform the necessary functions. Thus, if you want results you must develop the people you depend upon. To develop others, you must provide truthful feedback. People who are not performing up to expectations deserve honest feedback now. Most leaders/managers prefer to avoid this circumstance, so they hold back too long, cheating the person of a chance to learn and improve performance. A striving community needs everyone on board doing their best work and a continuous improvement feedback circle can help everyone perform at their best.

Throughout the U.S. there are excellent examples of local leaders rising up, demanding that conditions change, disrupting the status quo, and using their influence to energize community support. These leaders decided that the status quo was unacceptable and shared results across the community would, as one definition of economic development says, create new wealth.

Leadership often involves vision. The Bible says in Proverbs 29:18, "Without vision, the people perish." A vision is an ideal and unique image of a community's future. John F. Kennedy's vision during the space race with Russia was to have Americans travel to the moon and thus a nation's goal was born from a leader's vision. "In essence, leaders become great not because

---

49 Portion in Fast Company, October/November 1996

of their power but because of their ability to empower others."
(John Maxwell)

Good to Great

In Jim Collins' book "**Good to Great**"[50] he says that the vast majority of communities never become great, precisely because the vast
majority become quite good – and that is their main problem. In
essence, a variation on The Peter Principle[51], communities reach
their plateau and never move to a greater plateau.

There are some excellent leadership lessons from "*Good to Great*"
that apply to communities who want to move beyond their current
level of competitiveness.

- **"Good is the enemy of great"** as a majority of communities
  tend to simply settle for good when it comes to schools, governments, regulations, and economic development.
- Striving communities confront the brutal facts about their
  community and situation, yet never lose faith – facts are better than dreams! Facts are the starting point upon which
  one can build.
- Just like companies, striving communities require Level
  5 leaders – humble on a personal level but possessing a
  great deal of drive and desire to succeed. Only people who
  believe in themselves generate believers. You may have
  seen what appears to be arrogance and swagger working,
  but that will not last. To have followers you must believe --
  in yourself, in what you're doing, and in the capabilities of those who report to you. You also must believe in

---

50   Collins, Jim, *Good to Great: Why Some Companies Make the Leap and Others
Don't*, Harper Collins, October 16, 2001.
51   Peter, Laurence and Hull, Raymond, *The Peter Principle: Why Things Always
Go Wrong*, William Morrow and Company, 1969.

yourself enough to be able to take criticism without getting defensive.

- First Who...Then What – *"Look, I don't really know where we should take this bus. But I know this much: If we get the right people on the bus, the people in the right seats, and the wrong people off the bus, then we'll figure out how to take it someplace great."*[52]

- The right people don't need to be tightly managed or fired up; they will be self-motivated by the inner drive to produce the best results.

- One cannot become a great community leader until you are a great communicator – communicate from the perspective of the other people – the ones you want to get on the bus. It has been said, "The single biggest problem in communication is the illusion that it has taken place."[53] Think about that for a second.

- When trying to influence community stakeholders, engage in dialogue and debate, not coercion – forced participation will normally fail.

- God gave us two ears and one mouth to listen twice as much as we speak[54]. Pastor Andy Stanley says that "leaders who

---

52 Collins, Jim, *Good to Great: Why Some Companies Make the Leap and Others Don't*, page 13.

53 Commonly attributed to George Bernard Shaw on several places on the Internet. According to Quote Investigator, Inc. the earliest use in print is in a Fortune article, *"Is Anybody Listening?"* by William Hollingsworth Whyte, Start Page 77, Quote Page 174, Published by Time, Inc., New York., September 1950. Source: https://quoteinvestigator.com/2014/08/31/illusion/#note-9667-1

54 In sales, the correct ratio is 4 to 1 – God gave you two eyes, two ears, and one mouth. Start relationships with questions paying close attention to the other person. Learn what is important to them, identify their objectives and what they want to achieve. Know how what you are offering fits with what they want to buy. Now you are ready to sell. The more the people you want to influence talk, the smarter you become.

don't listen will eventually be surrounded by people who have nothing to say."

- Great communities are proactive rather than reactive – getting ahead of the issue rather than managing from behind the issue. Lead, follow, or get out of the way!

- A Culture of Discipline – *"Much of the answer to the question of 'good to great' lies in the discipline to do whatever it takes to become the best with carefully selected arenas and then to seek continual improvement from there."*[55]

- What is the one big thing that your community needs to accomplish? Collins talks about the fox and the hedgehog. The fox knows many things, but the hedgehog knows one big thing. Hedgehogs perceive a complex situation/challenge with clarity and consistency by employing a single idea or basic principle that guides, organizes, and unifies.

- "The Flywheel" refers to momentum and its importance in pushing a community in a certain direction. As you keep pushing, you'll build up momentum to help overcome the obstacles that are sure to come. Momentum is built a little bit at a time – it's not a dramatic, revolutionary change but constant, diligent work. Sports provide an excellent example of how momentum can influence attitudes and drive a team toward victory. The "Big Mo" is a real part of sports *and* economic development.

Motivate then Activate

What does it take to motivate and thus activate local leaders? Leaders can be energized if they realize their lives and businesses are dependent on how well their community is doing. Secondly, they are motivated through the belief that the organization(s) they

---

55 Collins, Jim, *Good to Great: Why Some Companies Make the Leap and Others Don't*, Chapter 6, Harper Collins, October 16, 2001.

support and in which they become engaged are truly helping move the community in a direction that fits their personal and business interests.

In the Pareto principle[56] most things in life are not distributed evenly. This 80-20 rule applied to economic development says that a relatively small percentage of folks in any community stimulate most of the subsequent decisions and effects. This is also known as the law of the vital few.

In the case of economic development, it is the principle that a vital few of an organization's stakeholders account for 80% of the results. From a community standpoint, it may also demonstrate that only the vital few are involved in decisions and actions that impact the 80%. The concept of leaderfulness suggests that the more of the community that can become involved in decisions on *how to grow* the community, the more successful the efforts will be. The goal should be to get above the 20% active participation rate.

With a board of directors, how can the leadership burden be shifted to the entire board rather than just the "vital few?" As strategic plans are developed to improve the community, what's the process to involve as many constituents as possible?

This calls for the organization's leaders to listen carefully and value the opinions of others. This helps maintain sensitivity to the world around you and deserves your careful reflection. If the decision is to go in another direction, use evidence to support the decision.

Once you identify the benefits of incorporating diverse opinions then Joe Raelin in *Creating Leaderful Organizations*[57] can help.

---

56 Named for Vilfredo Pareto who introduced it in 1906. It is applied to <u>all</u> <u>types</u> of economic and social factors – e.g., 20% of the inputs/business organizations cause 80% of the outputs/employment.

57 John Raelin, *Creating Leaderful Organizations: How to Bring Out Leadership in Everyone*, Barret-Koehler, 2003

He discusses the concept of leaderfulness in four "c's" – concurrent, collective, collaborative, and compassionate.

- Concurrent – may be the most revolutionary because it suggests that there can be more than one leader operating at the same time on the same subject. By sharing power, success can be enhanced by everyone working together.
- Collective – The community is not dependent on one individual to mobilize but collective action can emerge from multiple stakeholders especially when key decisions must be made.
- Collaborative – The leaderful approach seeks to engage in a public dialogue in which all constituents willingly express their beliefs and values. Everyone should feel comfortable advocating a point of view that they believe can contribute to the common good of the community.
- Compassionate – All sectors of the community are valued regardless of background or social standing. All viewpoints are considered whether or not they conform to prevailing views, thus preserving the dignity of others.

To move a community from fair to good to great begins with internal community drive. What are our community core values and real aspirations? In essence, what do we stand for? What do we really want to accomplish? What's driving us? Great communities are internally driven and externally aware.

King Solomon warns against "...chasing after the wind." We don't need tasks that are in reality meaningless, void of purpose. Ironically, today so many people complain about boredom when we live in an age of ever-changing technology, 200+ television channels, and countless outdoor pursuits. The word boredom didn't appear in our language until the Industrial Age, about the time modern forms of entertainment began to evolve.

When focusing on communities, leaders must work against boredom and chasing after the wind. Or, as Don Quixote taught us – tilting after windmills.[58]

Just like a growing company, a community should acknowledge and address its internal challenges before it can successfully market to the world. What can Community "A" do better than anyone else in the region that matches what companies need now or in the future? Life throws a lot at us but the ultimate responsibility for a community's destiny lies **within the community**. Remember, demographics do not always determine destiny. However, it takes disruptive thinking to overcome demographic challenges.

Leadership does not need to be a lonely road. For many communities, success may ultimately depend on a range of leaders who play their part - who help define an opportunity through the eyes of the broad community. Through a spirit of collective purpose, broad leadership, and unique assets, communities can deliver extraordinary performance.

Many economic development programs begin and end with attracting industries to expand or relocate to their community. With this approach, they have defined the challenge as a need for jobs. But often, they realize the real goal is to create prosperity or new wealth for the community. **The redefinition forces the community to go beyond simply recruiting jobs because job attraction may or may not bring the desired prosperity. The redefinition requires a different approach to quality job creation – a broader definition of economic development that includes entrepreneurship, innovation, retail, existing industry expansion, as well as attraction. New wealth for the community should be the goal rather than just creating jobs.**

The Economic Developer as Disruptive Leader and Change Agent

---

58 Miguel de Cervantes, *Don Quixote*, Published 1605, by Francisco de Robles.

The focus of the professional economic developer is normally on achieving results that are aligned with the overall character of the community. Successful economic development is not for the faint-hearted. It is a serious business that requires serious people. Because the pace of work is fast and often uncontrolled, it requires an ability to learn quickly and thoroughly while continually recognizing and adapting to changing conditions.

The professional is often hired to manage the community's economic development process and thus has to communicate and motivate both private and elected leaders plus the organization's staff. The EDA board should allow the professional to manage the process under a set of goals and accountability measures. With new wealth generation and local initiatives, the economic developer is normally the quarterback employing initiative, innovation, creativity, motivation, problem-solving, and the confidence to handle a variety of challenges. (See Appendix, The Role of the Economic Development Quarterback.)

The evolving economic development professional incorporates change and disruption as a part of his/her role. With the ultimate goal to create new wealth in a community, the professional must assess the community's competitive situation to determine what needs to be changed or improved to achieve success. In essence, the economic developer becomes a **change agent.**

In a community, change is often difficult, but the alternative might be fatal. Across America there are communities and some major cities that did not adapt to changing times or did not address the emerging challenges that threatened them with economic upheaval or even stagnation. Change is the new normal for leadership success and all leaders, especially professional economic developers, should embrace the inevitability of change. In today's technological world, change is happening at a pace unseen in our lifetimes and will continue at an accelerated pace.

Therefore, part of the puzzle is to prioritize what to tackle first, second, third, and so forth. Where do I put my priorities?

One site consultant said that if professional economic developers are not looking/thinking ten years ahead, they are already behind. The world of job creation is evolving at a very rapid pace.

The economic developer is charged with growing the community and creating new wealth. If the community is lacking vital elements for successful wealth generation, then it is incumbent for the professional to work within the agency to address impediments. In other words, take responsibility for addressing and resolving weaknesses – three distinct choices: lead, convene, or support. Non-action is not acceptable.

The book and movie *Moneyball*[59] teach that winning support for innovative solutions, even for a small market baseball team competing with the big city, rich franchises might be painful, but can actually work if articulated and employed diligently over time. With change, we have to be patient yet persistent. Communicate compelling reasons for change and innovative strategies so that both stakeholders and constituents become your partners.

In today's very competitive world, communities should not rest on the acceptance of existing realities. Rather, the economic developer and the EDA leadership should merge their visions for a better community with agreement on the vital areas that require attention and action.

Ultimately, stakeholders and local leaders should perceive that the economic development professional is helping establish and achieve the community's expectations even if the professional has

---

59 Michael Lewis, *Moneyball: The Art of Winning an Unfair Game*, W.W. Norton & Co. March 17, 2003; Movie: *Moneyball*, Director Bennett Miller, screenplay by Stan Chervin with Steven Zaillian and Aaron Sorkin, Columbia Pictures, September 2011.

to disrupt the status quo through gently pushing toward attainable goals. The objective is to create a favorable environment within the organization and the community for consensus on the direction that leads to quality job creation.

In addition to leader, change agent, disrupter, and facilitator, the professional should also help educate the local leadership and the community on the process and value of new wealth creation through quality job creation. Both stakeholders and elected officials should constantly be learning in order to excel and keep up with the competition. The EDA director should take responsibility for designing an appropriate learning process for elected officials, staff, and community stakeholders understanding that all have specific roles in the process. Within that concept, the community has a much better chance of becoming a leaderful community.

Part of the process is setting realistic timelines for accomplishing goals. No community rises or falls overnight. Prepare the community for the process and set some goals that can be accomplished quickly. People want to see results to stay energized.

A calculated learning process might include forums, comparable city visits, workshops, dissemination of key articles/books, and other opportunities to enlighten the knowledge base. Engaging local leadership in the process increases support for and participation in community efforts to expand prosperity.

At the end of the day, the professional economic developer should embrace her or his leadership role as community change agent – using their position to influence areas that might keep a community from successfully creating new, quality jobs. Remember, lead, convene, or support.

CHAPTER 7

PRODUCT, PRODUCT, PRODUCT

Project Penguin reminded everyone how important the decision to create a Bedford County industrial park with four-lane and rail access had been to the region's job creation efforts. Several years before he became EDA chairman, Roger Barnett assisted David's efforts to get an industrial park funded and infrastructure committed.

The local elected officials were slow to grasp the necessity to provide product but once they fully understood the importance, things moved quite quickly.

The last Council meeting before voting on government funding in support of an industrial park attracted a packed council chamber. David's volunteer team had done much to seed the necessity of a prepared site with the public, but there were still naysayers who pressured the five council members.

David presented a well-reasoned defense, but actually turned it into an effective offense replaying his athletic days that a great offense can trump a good defense. The vote was four to one in favor of moving ahead. Now Project Penguin reinforced that everyone made a good decision because it was likely, without an adequate site that met the prospect's needs, Bedford would not have been in the competition.

David and his team knew that Bedford's response to the RFP and a ready site helped generate a site visit that kept them in the hunt.

C ommon sense and numerous studies clearly indicate that having a prepared product that fits a particular project or industry sector are key criteria for site selection.

Since economic development is the process of elimination, an available qualified product(s) gets a community in the game more often while the lack of required product most likely eliminates from the start. There are examples of successful efforts based on available raw land that meet the size requirements, but they are few and far between.

What is product? Many requests for proposals (RFP) come with specific building and/or site requirements. An RFP requesting a 300-acre prepared site, or a 50,000 square foot existing building clearly defines what product is required and, most often, whether a community will be able to compete.

Many communities have invested in an industrial park that offers highway, rail, and/or port access and the necessary utilities. Some sites are certified which can be, in theory, developed quicker because the necessary ingredients for a company are in place or easily accessible – e.g., utilities, regulations, access roads, and environmental assessments. In other words, the necessary due diligence has been completed.

With no national standards in place, certification is a nebulous term. Some firms specialize in site certification and have a reputation for thoroughness that is generally accepted by consultants and companies. Some communities take a less expensive path and "self-certify." Companies and consultants normally prefer a third-party verification, believing that self-certification is a red flag, conflict of interest.

Full certification addresses zoning, soil, parcel configuration, size, utilities, road access, rail service, and numerous environmental issues. Therefore, certification can often take weeks or months. Several state agencies, private organizations, and consulting firms offer site certification.

There are intermediate steps that some communities use short of certification. These steps include an evaluation of sites for certain industry sectors, providing due diligence upfront, and putting the community in a position to expand to a full certification process or even construction at a later date. The intermediate steps identify what costs, time, and hurdles will be required to get the necessary utilities, access roads, etc. to the site and what environmental challenges lie ahead. These are questions that will need to be addressed in either the RFP or at the initial site visit.

It is critical that either the economic development organization or government agency have control of the property or, at least, a binding option. Consultants and companies want to be sure that, when you make a site available, you have control of the site.

Trust but Verify

During the Reagan years, the term "trust but verify" became an American lexicon. When a consultant has a client that is depending on his/her evaluation of a site or building, the consultant cannot take key information at face value. Most consultants will do their own due diligence no matter who put the seal of approval on the site. Remember, the best surprise is no surprise.

To an economic developer, site consultant, or prospective company, a "shovel-ready" site indicates available (with ironclad control), developable property that is served, or easily served by utilities and infrastructure. Shovel ready is not necessarily certified by an agency or firm but is ready for development. Some major projects have chosen shovel ready sites over certified sites and worked with the various government agencies to provide the necessary utilities and infrastructure.

With shovel ready or raw land sites, the economic development agencies need to be ready to answer tough questions about costs and length to get a site prepared for construction. Many state site inventory databases won't even include sites (and shouldn't) without key information including control of the property which is an essential element of available sites. If the project decision-maker pulled the trigger, can the property be delivered within the time required, and at what price?

Spec Buildings

Some communities have invested in spec buildings either alone or in partnership with a developer or utility in recognition that companies or site consultants might require an existing building for project consideration. The approach is to build a shell that can easily be converted into a company's specific requirements.

There are questions and risks that should be addressed before pulling the trigger on a spec building. Who will build? What size? Who will own? Who will control? Who will market? Who's accountable and will make decisions about price/terms? A spec building must be properly constructed to the needs of some likely targets of interest, strategically located, well maintained, and effectively marketed. Throughout America, there are winning success stories that would not have happened without a spec building in place. However, there are also spec buildings sitting idle without a chance of a client.

If a community believes a spec building is a workable option, consider all risks, all opportunities, and enter into it with eyes wide open.

Some cities/communities have invested in property and buildings to enhance their competitive negotiating positions. While being creative from an incentive standpoint, elected officials should protect their responsibility to the taxpayer to get something of value when the property/building is used for a job creation project. Should something nefarious happen to the new company within a specified amount of time, the land and assets should revert back to the funding entity. It is important that elected officials be able to defend a decision to use government property as an inducement/investment for a for-profit company locating in the community rather than as corporate welfare. Good and ironclad clawback and reversion provisions[60] help ensure a deal that is good for the taxpayer and good for the company.

Many communities have former industrial or commercial buildings that, with the right deal, could be included in the community's available inventory. Other fortunate communities have been deeded buildings or sites by private companies for the express purpose of attracting a new business. These are valuable assets that often meet the needs of a prospect. The economic development agency and government entities should explore creative ways to get control of these valuable assets with a plan to turn them back into tax-generating properties.

As outlined throughout this book, elected officials have certain special roles in the job creation process: incentive decisions, responsible regulations, education/workforce excellence, safety, quality of life, and infrastructure. Well thought out government-controlled

---

60 Clawbacks are placed in agreements to make sure taxpayers' development subsidies pay off. The company receiving benefits must perform at a specified level or pay the money utilized back.

sites and buildings can be a key responsibility that gets a community in the competitive game for wealth creation.

For every local economic development organization, a key to success is getting community leaders on a common page in terms of community direction, resources, targets, quality of life, performance metrics, and infrastructure. Be sure to also keep them up to date. Change will be more frequent in our future than it was in our past.

CHAPTER 8

COOPETITION

"Mr. Gorbachev – Tear Down This Wall"
—*President Ronald Reagan*

As with almost any community in America, natural silos form caus-
ing the community's leadership unanticipated challenges. The EDA
chairman, Roger Barnett, began his tenure working to tear down
walls and build a cooperative approach to the challenges facing
Bedford.

The chamber had been around for decades, so Roger worked
with the community's business membership organization to do an
honest appraisal of the roles of the two organizations. Roger and the
chamber chairman requested David at the EDA and Sue Chambers
at the Chamber begin a series of joint meetings to make sure, from
a staff standpoint, every aspect of growing the community was cov-
ered and each staff member had his/her distinct lane.

Still, there were intangible but real walls between the agencies
in Bedford. With that realization, David and Sue began a partnership that would eventually lead to creative approaches to community and economic development. As they became comfortable with
the separate agencies but common purpose, they began to make sure

their leadership teams shared optimism for the future. EDA chairman Barnett led the effort to work seamlessly among the two boards of directors.

With those tough years under their belts, the cooperative approach that was taking shape really became critical as the community organizations sat around the table to hammer out a Bedford recovery strategy. Sue and David led the unified discussions and their selflessness became infectious.

The EDA was also part of a five-county consortium that had been formed to pool resources and market the region to decision-makers. For the past two years, this attempt at regional cooperation had been rocky to say the least as trust levels among the partners were tested. Some were questioning whether the alliance had been formed on solid pillars or quicksand.

Project Penguin had come to Bedford's EDA directly from the state and Bedford was the only community in their regional partnership to be included in the project RFP. David knew, when this became public, there would be some bruised egos and questions to the state about why Bedford and not us.

A lot of change was going on and local elections were just around the corner. Plus, communities were struggling to find the secret formula to the devastating pandemic. As David reminded himself almost every day, local economic development was an unpredictable animal.

I t was around 2 p.m. in front of the Brandenburg Gate in the Federal Republic of Germany in 1987 that President Ronald Reagan challenged Soviet leader Mikhail Gorbachev to tear down the Berlin Wall. Reagan's speech is credited as a driving force leading to East and West Germany reuniting.

Steve Jobs addressed the issue of walls when he said, "Tear down walls, build bridges, light fires."[61]

Walls have always been with us, both tangible and intangible. Maybe we don't have a 5,500-mile Great Wall like China which took more than 200 years to construct beginning in the Ming Dynasty. But, walls exist all around us. From an economic development standpoint, it is the intangible walls within and around cities, counties, regions, and states that cause the most trouble. Imaginary walls often define boundaries and may impede the ability to maximize true potential.

What is interesting is that these boundaries are mostly meaningless when it comes to the best location for a new or expanded facility. Businesses want to maximize business interests whether they stay inside one particular boundary or not.

Coopetition
There is a relatively new term that challenges the notion of building or maintaining walls. **Coopetition** emerges when business competitors cooperate on a particular project or product knowing that they will also compete against each other in the marketplace. Competitors collaborate in the hope of mutually beneficial results especially when they do not believe that with a "go it alone" strategy they have the competitive advantage they need. It happens quite often in the automotive industry as rivals, for example, share research and development costs on a new engine knowing that the engines will be placed in competing automobiles.

There is an even more dramatic example involving two Japanese automotive giants. In 2017, Toyota and Mazda announced that they would build a joint U.S assembly plant with separate production lines under one roof. While sharing assembly facilities, the

---

61 George Beahm, *I, Steve: Steve Jobs in His Own Words*, Agate B2,page 61, October 19, 2011.

different autos will eventually compete in the marketplace. That is coopetition.

There's the old saying "The sum is greater than the total of its parts." Helen Keller once said, "Alone we can do so little; together we can do so much."[62] But Andrew Carnegie may have nailed it from an economic development standpoint: "Strength is derived from unity. The range of our collective vision is far greater when individual insights become one."

Sometimes lessons from children are especially on the mark. When you look at a child's crayon box you find all types of crayons. Some are sharp, some are pretty, a few dull, while others are bright, some have weird names, but they all have to live in the same box.

Alliances – Enter with Your Eyes Wide Open
Unfortunately, employing the concept of coopetition in economic development is harder than it sounds. It is difficult for competing organizations or communities to make it work. In fact, the failure rate of strategic alliances is estimated as high as sixty percent. For the mayor of one community to watch the mayor of another community announce a new job creation project places special pressure on the concept of tearing down walls in order to work better together. "Why did they get the project and we didn't?"

A strategic alliance is a formal arrangement between two or more entities for the purpose of ongoing cooperation and mutual gain. For an alliance to work, communities need to clearly define where they are working together and where they are competing. There should be an understood stated purpose to the alliance, which is agreed upon by all partners as a good, strategic fit.

---

62 Spoken by Helen Keller in a speech as told in 1980, Helen and Teacher: *The Story of Helen Keller and Anne Sullivan Macy* by Joseph P. Lash, Chapter: On the Vaudeville Circuit, Start Page 487, Quote Page 489, A Merloyd Lawrence Book: Delacorte Press/Seymour Lawrence, New York.

One of the nation's oldest regional organizations Metro Denver Economic Development Corporation decided to adopt a Code of Ethics[63] that "represents the standards that each member supports and practices in its daily conduct of business." In its Preamble, the organization underscores that the Metro Denver EDC "...was founded on the respect and trust of its members." All members sign the Code of Ethics indicating their support for the rules and spirit of coopetition of the region.

Embedded throughout a successful alliance is a strong level of trust among the partners. "Let's just create an alliance, it'll be a great thing," sounds good but is doomed to fail without the proper safeguards, rules, and principles. Here are some guidelines and truisms:

- Define potential partnering territories – does it make strategic and geographic sense to join together? Which industry or local targets should find the territory appealing?
- Define and accept the "what's in it for me" factor. Everyone wants to know the answer to that question even though they may not like the answer.
- Address the issue of relinquishing some or all control – quite often this is an underlying cause of failure and a roadblock to a successful alliance. "Who's giving up what and who's getting what?"
- Know the kind of cultures and personalities within the partnering groups – keep your friends close and your competitors closer.
- Clearly state and agree on the purpose of an alliance to ensure there is a strong strategic reason for collaboration. Can we accomplish the same objectives alone? If so, there may not be the need to partner. Remember, creating an alliance just because it sounds good is not a valid reason.

---

63 http://www.metrodenver.org/about/partners/code-of-ethics/

- Define lines of collaboration and competition – for instance, we may just collaborate on marketing but compete on everything else.
- State a well-defined value proposition for the alliance and be sure there is transparency and broad representation re: decisions, finances, and accountability
- Sometimes a rivalry like Friday Night Football can affect the success or failure of collaboration – sounds silly, doesn't it – but often it's very real.
- Have an exit strategy – just in case.

The failure rate for alliances is high. The most common root cause is a **lack of trust** among the partners. Too often, egos and personal issues interfere with the business purpose of an alliance emphasizing the need to evaluate potential partners before advancing too far.

Walls can divide a community's efforts and impede chances for successful job creation. But alliances, with proper buy-in, structure, and safeguards can allow smaller communities/counties an enhanced way to compete.

Peter Drucker, known by many as "the inventor of modern management," said that innovation and value are more commonly generated in networks. With that being said, economic development organizations and communities need to carefully evaluate the upside and downside to strategic partnerships and coopetition before entering into regional alliances. But it is an exercise that could pay huge dividends if handled correctly and makes sense for everyone involved.

Over the past decade, the Charleston, South Carolina region has seen dramatic growth in its three contiguous counties – Charleston, Dorchester, and Berkeley counties. Three cities in the region rank in the top 10 "boomtowns" in America according to a 2019 study by SmartAsset.

Charleston ranked No. 8, Mt. Pleasant ranked third and North Charleston ranked ninth. The region is a growing technology hub[64] and is the only place in the world with multiple automotive plants and an airplane assembly plant - Mercedes-Benz Sprinter vans and Boeing's east coast airplane assembly plant in North Charleston and Volvo automobiles in Berkeley County.

Intangible Walls
Within a community, intangible walls exist right under our noses: racial, financial, generational, religious, political, power, and territorial. Unseen walls, yet still real walls, can actually cause more damage than those that are easily visible.

Robert Frost's poem *Mending Wall* describes walls and includes this oft-quoted line "Good fences make good neighbors."[65] Many have tried to explain Frost's meaning, recognizing that the act of repairing the wall forces neighbors to work together. One wise old teacher explained that in order to mend fences following a harsh winter, the neighbors worked to mend the fences between their properties, and they would meet and talk to each other as they worked together toward a common goal.

In an exchange on *West Wing*, the hit TV show about a fictional president and his staff, Donna and Josh are debating the real meaning of Robert Frost's poem. Donna finally says that Frost wanted us to understand that "...boundaries are what alienate us from one another."[66]

---

64 Three counties working together in aerospace, automotive, and advanced technology.

65 Robert Frost, Mending Wall, published by David Nutt in 1914. Available: https://www.poetryfoundation.org/poems/44266/mending-wall

66 The West Wing is an American serial political drama television series created by Aaron Sorkin that aired on NBC from September 22, 1999 to May 14, 2006.

The teacher may have nailed the challenge we face with tangible and intangible walls. First, there is the recognition of an existing wall. Second, there is the need to repair those parts of the wall that impede progress. Thirdly, when repairs are a joint project, there is the opportunity to meet and talk together about common goals and challenges. But, fourthly and more importantly, there may be good reason to just tear the wall down. In Robert Frost's poem, remember, one neighbor was trying to get the other neighbor to take down the fence – it wasn't needed anymore.

Unseen walls too often impede communication and progress, i.e., the walls in an office, between faiths, among people, in schools, and among governments. Sometimes there are walls between business organizations as each competes for power and territory. Identifying intangible walls, acknowledging their existence, and taking steps to either tear down the walls or, at least, mitigate their impact is a step that agents of economic development need to take. Most importantly, a community's walls and boundaries mean nothing to a new manufacturing plant unless it affects their successful operations. For instance, they don't care that the site rests in two different counties or communities – they just want seamless regulations and support.

CHAPTER 9
A GOOD DEAL FOR THE TAXPAYER AND THE COMPANY

With Project Penguin assignments made, everyone left the meeting and headed to separate corners to begin putting together their part of the response. From the RFP, it was apparent that four criteria would drive the final decision: a skilled workforce, quality of life, the right site, and competitive incentives.

Bedford had really focused on education over the past three years becoming an ACT workforce certified community[67]. David and his team understood that talent and infrastructure were now the two leading criteria in most site searches, but incentives always lurked in the shadows.

With a seasoned elected official on the EDA board, the infrastructure challenges in Bedford found a receptive ear as she began to understand the needs companies and site consultants were outlining. The site deficiencies had slowly seeped into debate at commission meetings, especially at budget time. It was clear there were some gaps in site inventory that needed filling in order to truly

---

67 Industry-recognized workforce-ready certifications are available if a community is willing to make and keep the commitment.

compete for some of the community's targeted prospects, especially major projects.

In the shadows was the subject of incentives. For years, Bedford discussed and debated the necessity of incentives and whether it was good public business.

David and Betsy brought to the Commission several years ago the concept of a cost-benefit analysis process to help define a reasoned incentive response vs. an overly aggressive proposal. Even the local newspaper wrote an editorial supporting appropriate incentives that brought the community a good ROI.

In the mid-90s, the Commission had been "burned" by a start-up that had gone belly-up after receiving cash incentives upfront. It took some education, some rough headlines and a new process to get the Commission to a point of accepting appropriate incentives again as a necessary role in job creation competition. David and Betsy worked hard to restore trust in the process and they were about to find out if all their work would pay off with Project Penguin, especially now that the city and county coffers were depleted because of store, business, retail, and factory closings during the pandemic shutdown. They would really have to make a strong ROI case for Project Penguin if they were to advance to the next stage.

A t the turn of the 20th Century, Fantus Consulting began to grow and spread the early concept of site consulting across the U.S. Fantus was a pioneer of site selection with the first recorded U.S. state incentivized project in Mississippi.

Hugh Lawson White[68] was mayor of Columbia, Mississippi, in 1929 with one eye on bigger political fish within the state. That year, Fantus and White collaborated to land the Reliance

---

68   Mississippi History Now, David Sansing, 2004, *Economic Development in the 1930s: Balance Agriculture with Industry*, By Connie Lester, http://

Manufacturing Company, which was an early version of the growing textile industry in the South.

Columbia raised the requested $85,000 to pay for the plant and six years later White was elected governor of Mississippi, running on his fame as an aggressive industrial recruiter. White led Mississippi to create Industrial Revenue Bonds (IRBs) which several other southern states quickly copied. IRBs became a heated issue about twenty years later with congressional attempts to curtail or kill the tax-free bonds. Strong southern congressional leaders beat back the attack until Congress finally regulated them in 1968.

The Fantus/Mississippi project was one of the early projects in the long-running, incentives debate for recruiting and expanding industry. Today, there is a robust sector of site selection consultants who represent the interests of companies in search of expansion or new sites where incentives typically play a role.

The long-running incentives debate continues today with a 2012 negative series in *The New York Times*[69] and books railing against the perceived unsavory methods site consultants use to secure local and state incentives. A growing number of elected officials term it "corporate welfare" and object to any form of incentives. In 2016, one senior elected state official in a key southern state stated that any money spent on economic development is "bad."

The 2018 Amazon HQ2 project that finally named northern Virginia and New York's Long Island as co-winners renewed a vigorous debate about a very wealthy company pitting 238 cities against each other to "jack up the incentives." Many of the competing locales threw generous incentives at the company for the 50,000 employees or new jobs project. The very

---

www.mshistorynow.mdah.ms.gov/articles/224/economic-development-in-the-1930s-balance-agriculture-with-industry

69   Louise Story, Tiff Fehr And Derek Watkins, "*The United States of Subsidies: A series examining business incentives and their impact on jobs and local economies.*" *New York Times*, December 2012.

public competition demonstrated the degree to which communities will compete for one of the largest projects in history.

Following the selection of co-winners, the public backlash over incentives and excluding certain elected officials from the negotiating process caused Amazon to abandon the New York site. Fingers were pointed in all directions, but the breakdown exposed the strong feelings about incentives or corporate welfare as locals termed it, in some locales.

The Role of the Site Selection Consultant

In the world of today's rough and tumble site selection, professional consultants serve a very useful purpose in the process. By and large, today's site consultant is a professional intermediary between the prospect and locations under consideration. With a definition of economic development as the process of elimination, consultants help companies whittle down the list of potential sites to a manageable few so a reasoned final decision can be made. Quite often, a lot of good communities are eliminated without ever getting a site visit as discussed throughout this book. For example, the Amazon HQ2 project received 238 proposals but only a handful received a site visit.

Site consultants are a fact of economic development life and the wise professional economic developer will work to understand the rules of engagement. There is a healthy tension between the consultant and local professional that might be paraphrased based on Scripture: "the lion and the lamb may lie down together but the lamb isn't going to get much sleep."

Many studies show that, in the scheme of things and depending on who is being polled, incentives fall toward the top or middle of a list of important locational factors. But one axiom seems to hold true, incentives never make a bad site good. However, they can make a good site better. In addition, incentives come at the end of the site selection process when the final negotiation between a very few remaining sites compete for a favorable location decision from the company.

Incentives often get the most press and attention but, according to *Site Selection Magazine's* annual survey[70], the elimination factors throughout the process relate more toward skilled/educated workforce, access to markets, transportation, a suitable building/site, raw materials, infrastructure, and an overall good quality of life. It is the responsibility of the team managing a project to determine exactly what elimination factors are at play on any given project because they will vary from project to project.

The wise, competitive community has moved away from free-for-all giveaways and "we'll take any jobs" mentality to a carefully analyzed package that addresses incentives in concert with other key issues such as wage level and company investment. Elected officials and economic developers should always remember that, in the end, they have direct "say so" in the selection process and, therefore, in the level of incentives. A good cost-benefit analysis on each project can help local decision-makers make good decisions on what should be offered based on the resulting benefits the company has committed to the project.

Two rules of thumb are applicable:

- Fashion a deal that is good for the taxpayer and good for the company and
- No deal is better than a bad deal for both the community and the company – but especially the community.

Cost-Benefit Analysis

As communities begin to define the ingredients for an incentive package, some believe that incentives are akin to corporate welfare, fraught with unnecessary "giveaways" to companies that don't deserve or need it. The use of incentives can be a very important

---

70   Site Selection Magazine's *Site Selection Survey*, January, 2018. https://siteselection.com/

part of the response package. Responses have evolved but are normally based on a few key deciding factors:

- Level of capital investment the project brings to the community – how much are they spending or investing in the community?
- Number of quality jobs created and the average wage level for full-time employees. Some states and locales will not offer incentives if the prospect is not going to pay wages at least at the county's current average wage and some states require wages 25% or more above the current local average before state incentives kick-in. This approach ensures that new and expanding companies are truly helping grow the economy and maximize the ripple effect on other local businesses.[71]
- Ripple effect of direct jobs. In other words, calculate the financial impact of direct, induced, and indirect jobs on the community.
  - ○ **Direct Jobs** – direct employment at the plant or business
  - ○ **Indirect Jobs** – as a result of direct employment, additional workers are generated at businesses that supply goods or services to the main plant, i.e., suppliers
  - ○ **Induced Jobs** – new jobs created as a result of employees spending their wages in businesses, restaurants, etc. in town and around the region
- Some states/locales only provide discretionary monetary incentives to the prospect after the company has created the promised jobs and maintained the jobs for one, two, and three years – paying the incentives in equal amounts during a set maintenance period.

---

71 Some communities may view certain companies or business sectors desirable and grant local incentives even though their average wages do not meet certain thresholds.

These key factors should be included in a cost-benefit analysis which helps the local economic development organization justify the requested level of incentives and allows decision-makers to make a reasoned decision based on impact data for the project.

While the economic development organization (EDO) normally manages the cost-benefit analysis and site selection process for a community, the final incentive decision rests with the local/state elected officials – not the economic developer. The EDO gives elected officials "cover" until that magic moment when the stars align and everyone is ready to go on the record with a successful project decision.

As with any successful football team, there needs to be a great quarterback. In this case, site selection consultants prefer the EDO manage the process. This ensures one experienced point of contact throughout the process and professional responses at each stage of the project. But of course, in the end, the government agencies have final approval since they will be the ones standing at the announcement and ultimately facing voters.

Effective Negotiations

In almost every project, there are negotiating sessions that often set the stage for a final agreement or to just walk away. As with any deal, there are rules of engagement that should be followed, but the first rule is to prepare and prepare well. In most cases, the company and site consultant will be fully prepared so this interaction is not something to take lightly.

The first step in preparing for project negotiation is to gather as much information as possible on the prospective company, their decision team, and the site consultant. This should begin as soon as you determine the company and eventually the individuals involved. Remember, after greetings, start your in-person prospect interactions with questions. Everything you learn before the negotiation phase begins can be used in the negotiation.

In sports, you gather vital data on opponents so you can predict what they actually have, understand how they perceive you, and their most predictable plays. Listening and paying attention are extremely important tools in sports and business negotiations.

Once the professional EDO has done as much due diligence as it can, the community team, led by the quarterback, should develop a negotiating game plan prior to meeting with the prospective company and/or site consultant. It is important to agree on, hopefully, all of the following points:

- What is everyone's role on the community team? Roles may vary with different projects, communities, and cultures. Fully understand the cultural nuances to ensure each community team member understands their correct role and says the appropriate things. The quarterback for the project needs to define and communicate everyone's role so there isn't overlap and confusion.

- Who is the scribe? Be sure correct notes, decisions, and observations are recorded to help the community team assess what happened, what was decided, and next steps.

- No activity is more important in successful negotiations than planning. The local team should devote quality time to planning a negotiation approach and strategy.

- What is the goal for this negotiation session? You may gain some valuable intelligence by communicating directly with the site consultant before the session to ensure you are both on the same page in terms of expectations or at least understand where the gaps are located for the upcoming session.

- What is important to the prospect? Are there critical issues and why are they important? For every possible company interest, there usually exist several possible community positions that can satisfy it. From the first time you interact with the client, be inquisitive. Get as much of the story as possible because the more you learn about the prospect the better your community responses and ability to influence others will be.

- What is important to your team and the community? Have a scoring system that defines the most important issues for your community. Also, have a team understanding of what your "Reservation Price," or bottom line, is for the project. Your positions are something the team has discussed, agreed upon, and will be unveiled at strategically the best time. Also remember, in a successful negotiation both sides win on the things that matter the most to them.

- Aim high in your approach to the project. Michelangelo said that "the greatest danger for most of us is not that our aim is too high and we miss it, but that it is too low and we hit it."[72]

- A well-thought-out local package may have multiple options. This approach can signal cooperation and set a tone for the entire session. If at all possible, try to make concessions that do not cost tangible resources, i.e., cash, rather, employing value-add-ons to sweeten the package whenever possible.

- Stay away from an arms race mentality by trying to match the incentives a competing state/community offers. Some site consultants may use a strategy to get competing locations to up the ante by revealing certain incentives/CASH other states/locales are offering. "You must do X, Y, and Z to stay in the game!" Remember, if you decide to exceed your Reservation Price or bottom-line, do so with eyes wide

---

72 https://www.goodreads.com/quotes/557979-the-greatest-danger-for-most-of-us-is-not-that

open. What will the new requested incentives do to the project's cost-benefit analysis and economic impact on the community? Can you defend it when it's all said and done? Can the elected officials defend it to the public?

- Sometimes during certain negotiations, you may need to call a "timeout" for a community team side-bar discussion. This approach allows the team to assess the situation and make a value decision on what to accept/not accept and what strategies need to be employed as negotiations continue. Patience is a source of power in negotiation so know when to bargain and give concessions.

- Always use language that sends the signal "We're trying to help the company accomplish its goals." As Tom Cruise said to Cuba Gooding in the movie *Jerry Maguire*[73], "Help me help you."

- A Holiday Inn ad years ago stated: "The best surprise is no surprise." Somewhere in the discussions, be sure the company knows the timing for the government approval process, what is required from the company to make a local decision, and the steps toward a public announcement. A "timing" discussion will also identify any deadlines that the prospective company indicates must be met on their end. By everyone laying their cards on the table, it minimizes the opportunity of unnecessary surprises.

- A poster caption from World War II states the need for confidentiality: Loose Lips Sink Ships – they could lose a project too!

- Nothing is settled until everything is settled. Or as Yogi Berra famously said, "It ain't over until it's over."[74]

---

73 *Jerry McGuire*, written & directed by Cameron Crowe, released December 13, 1996, produced by Gracie Films and distributed by TriStar Pictures.
74 Yogi Berra, *Yogi Berra*, Workman Publishing, Inc., May 26, 2010.

The Incentives' Toolkit

States and locales generally have numerous incentive options to consider when vying for a project:

- Discretionary incentives – cash that can be used to close the deal or sweeten the pot.
- Statutory incentives – established by law or government regulation and usually based on the number of jobs/wages/capital investment. A growing trend exists to make these performance-based rather than upfront. In other words, the project has to meet certain job creation goals and maintain them before any incentives are distributed.
- Local incentives – can be in the form of cash, abatements, land, building, and/or infrastructure.
- Some states have special job credits or incentives for projects locating in rural counties.
- Sales/use tax exemptions – usually for a defined number of years and based on job creation/wages/investment.
- Creative real estate options/terms/financing – these are usually at the local level and involve government properties or buildings.
- Tax Increment Financing (TIF) – allocates future increases in property taxes from a designated area to pay for improvements within that defined area. It is usually triggered based on the investment by the project and the size of the proposed site. The "increment" in TIF is the enhanced property tax from the new infrastructure and buildings provided by the recruited industry. Also, the incentives used to recruit the industry will be paid by revenues from increased property values within the zone beyond what is presently generated. Additionally, property values may also rise outside the area, creating new revenue, and adding additional benefits to the region.[75]

75 SmartAsset, Amelia Josephson, *What is Tax Increment Financing?* December 12, 2019; https://smartasset.com/taxes/what-is-tax-increment-financing#q=TIF

- Workforce Training Provisions – varies from state to state but designed to identify and train both new workers and those currently employed.

A Slippery Slope

Some elected officials refer to incentives as corporate welfare without recognizing that, if done correctly, it is an investment in both the new company and the community as a whole.

Many states/locales have moved to performance-based incentives that require the new company to meet certain requirements before or as they are creating the jobs before incentives can be dispersed. Some communities may decide that up-front cash incentives are appropriate or necessary to either win the project or stay in the game.

Upfront CASH is a slippery slope that all too often comes back to bite one's posterior. Cash should only be used as an incentive under the strictest of terms with ironclad clawbacks and for the most financially strong companies. Government agencies should resist putting up-front cash incentives into a start-up operation because the percentages are just not in your favor. Remember: **No deal may be better than a bad deal.**

Wise EDOs do their research intelligence homework on prospective companies to make wise, calculated recommendations to local or state incentive granting agencies. It may be a D&B or other forms of research but the clear message is, do your homework!

If you know the competing states or communities, research their incentive programs to gain a sense of what the competition might be offering. You can also resurrect some of their past project deals to gain additional intelligence. Think of it as football coaches do prior to each game – they watch game film of the upcoming opponent to learn as much as possible about what to expect in their next game. **Preparation is 90% of performance.** Opposition research has become a well-known political term but the concept applies to economic development competition as well. It helps fashion a competitive but defensible incentive package.

Engaged elected officials will seek to understand the incentive process so that, when the EDO makes its project package recommendation, they are better prepared to make educated, informed decisions. While the professional EDO should manage the process and provide elected officials with the necessary information to make the best decisions, elected officials should also understand the important role they play preparing the community for successful economic development i.e. responsible regulations, adequate infrastructure, world-class education, low crime, affordable/available housing, and necessary city/county services.

Today's packages usually involve non-monetary incentives that can have a big impact on both expanding and recruited projects:

- Favorable regulatory climate for permitting and zoning/covenant variances – The states/communities that have trimmed the permitting process see more project activity than communities that give the perception of "hard to deal with," cumbersome, or not being business-friendly.
- Service after the sale – Serving as an ombudsman to investigate issues and run interference between the company and governments. Good EDOs provide **continuous interaction** with expanding and new companies to help ensure their success. This approach will pay dividends in so many ways long after the company locates or expands.
- University/College consulting – Utilizing the vast resources educational institutions have to support the broad definition of job creation – recruiting, commercial, entrepreneurial, existing industry expansion, and retail.
- Temporary space – Allowing companies ease of initial operations and fostering an attitude of partnership.

- Working to integrate new families into the community – A feel-good offer that, quite often, resonates with the company decision-makers.

Defending the Deal

Just as it is best for the EDO to quarterback each site selection process, it is also best to have one spokesperson for the incentive package – probably the EDO director. Let the elected officials take credit for the "win" and the economic developer outline the incentive package that helped secure the project.

Many communities/states hold the project announcement and the incentive package session with media on the same day but not at the same time. In that scenario, the "big news article or afternoon TV news" can focus on both the positives from the announcements and the benefits to the taxpayer vs. the community investment used to win the project.

It is best to separate the public celebration announcement of the new project from the session with news media about the project's incentives. Some tips for the media gaggle:

- Publicize the time for the media incentive session at the same time you notify the media of a pending project announcement. With that format, the media knows in advance that while the formal celebration announcement is going on they will also get the opportunity to discuss the incentive package later that day. This approach allows the media to write a complete article on the project and keeps your transparency intact. It also builds and reinforces trust with the media.
- Use a conference room where a PowerPoint can visually "frame" the importance/impact of the project as well as the incentives used to win the project. Focus on job creation, ripple effect on the local economy, average wages,

and investment by the new community partner. But, keep it simple. Clearly outline the economic impacts on the community.

- Walk through the summary with the media allowing for questions and discussion about the entire package/process/impact.
- If appropriate and practical, include a company spokesperson in the media session to be available for questions from the media but...
- Anticipate media questions and be ready with answers. Practice with your team to get it right! Treat it like preparing for a debate.
- Use the "front-page rule" – whatever you say during the media session, would you be OK seeing it on the front page of tomorrow's newspaper or leading the evening television news?

In today's economic development, incentives are a necessary part of the equation. They should never be taken lightly by any entity involved in the package and, if used properly, can be a key tool in competing for new jobs and investment. Also, remember the adage: Incentives should be good for the taxpayer AND the company.

CHAPTER 10

TALENT IS TODAY'S CURRENCY

At the Wee Diner early one Tuesday morning, the center table for lively debate on the subject de jour turned to education and the soaring unemployment predictions for the pandemic aftermath. Over weak coffee and scrambled eggs, the discussion centered on whether Bedford's students were as good as the next state's students or even the next county. Pride kicked in but it was a discussion heavily tainted in politics and where their grandchildren were going to find good jobs.

Charles Blass, approaching 80 years old, couldn't seem to understand the need for accelerated and rigorous studies, especially since many of the students, he thought, would stay in Bedford and follow their parents in the kind of jobs they had. When it was explained that Bedford had advanced manufacturing companies and wanted to attract more technology-driven companies to town, he waved his arms in surrender. He still didn't fully understand but conceded that it's a more competitive and complicated world than when he managed the Western Auto on Main Street.

In fact, one of the old gents around the table had just learned from his grandson that employers who fifty years ago only needed workers no matter whether they graduated from high school or not, now needed workers with both a high school degree and some type of post-secondary education or training. It was a different world than those old coots around the breakfast table understood.

The EDA and its partners had focused a lot of sweat equity in moving the local education system to join forces with the local community college and key local industries to help students begin to look at trades and certificates that would fit nicely with Bedford's existing and targeted industry base. But, now the local employment situation had changed and the once record low unemployment was predicted to extend well into double digits.

Part of the local recovery team's discussions centered around workforce and the impact the pandemic shutdown would have on current and future jobs. Before the Coronavirus, the EDA had a robust attraction strategy but that would surely be impacted – what industries and businesses would be the winners and fit their local demographics? Innovation, technology, and artificial intelligence were rapidly changing the job market before the pandemic and would certainly impact it now.

But everyone around the recovery team table knew they had to put the main focus on their local companies – be sure they knew their needs, especially when it came to workers. The education leaders needed to be at the table and ready to offer concrete suggestions. Good talent was truly today's economic development currency and the education leaders had to become active partners in making sure Bedford had ample currency in the workforce bank.

Education is the most powerful weapon to change the world![76] Please note, you have to use what you learn for it to have

---

76 Nelson Mandela, from a speech given at Madison Park High School, Boston, June 23, 1990.

value[77]. Based on most lists and experiences, it is either a major or the number one criterion for attraction, company expansions, and, too often, elimination.

States' and communities' global competitiveness depends on closing the skills gap if this nation is going to address the number of manufacturing jobs going unfilled. And now that once-favored manufacturing regions in Asia have experienced wage increases, cost rises in supply chain/logistics, and soaring energy costs, U.S. manufacturers are rethinking off-shore facilities. With baby boomers retiring in droves, estimates are that three to five million or more manufacturing jobs will be available in the U.S. over the next decade and beyond.

At the height of the last recession, 32% of manufacturers reported that they had jobs going unfilled because they could not find workers with the right skills. Eighty-four percent stated that K-12 school systems were doing an inadequate job of preparing students for the workforce.[78]

Some Truisms and Predictions:

- There was a recent trend that baby boomers have been retiring leaving holes in the workforce. Before the pandemic, the U.S. experienced record low unemployment and the skilled talent pipeline was not deep enough to fill workforce gaps. The jury is out as to how many laid-off or furloughed workers will be asked back post-pandemic but there is sure to be impacts on how many, what skills will be required, and which companies will be hiring.
- Before the pandemic, too many of today's workers were deficient in requisite skills especially as technology and robotics

---

77 One of the authors told students and practitioners alike: Knowledge increases the capacity to perform. The application of knowledge turns capacity into reality. Use what you learn.

78 *Roadmap to Education Reform for Manufacturers*, Manufacturing Institute. http://www.themanufacturinginstitute.org/~/media/736409933C084EECB2 A307E0814DF757.ashx

become greater players in advanced manufacturing and business in general. This is both a threat and an opportunity. Change agent economic developers should be partnering with education and workforce training to tackle deficiencies.

- Discussions with local industries will reveal future needs from both a workforce and a skills training standpoint. Keep that communication line wide open.
- As technology accelerates, new types of workers will be required with new skill sets – a high school diploma will no longer be sufficient to get the decent job it could command forty years ago. The pandemic recovery and high unemployment will present new pressures for even the most qualified workers.
- Unemployment rates do not give the complete picture of the available workforce and the impact from the pandemic. With the mandated national shut-down America experienced many workers at home for weeks. Therefore, unemployment rates alone won't capture everyone available and wanting work. Following the local numbers should be a key role for the economic development team because you must understand your workforce situation in order to help develop an effective local workforce strategy and articulate the workforce pipeline to a prospect.
- Technical and specific job training certificates for many are better financially in the long run than getting a four-year degree – and in many cases more satisfying. With certificates, jobs are often available immediately while those with four-year degrees may take years to fully capture their earning power.

Each growing community and region face the same questions in today's competitive economic development marketplace:

- Will my community have the necessary skilled workforce to meet the growing demand for employees in existing industries and those targeted for attraction?

- Is our community taking aggressive steps to provide the talent pipeline that will stay home for local jobs? Can we create jobs that will allow job commuters to return home? In some communities/counties, more than half the working population leaves the county each day for work. For the right job at home, commuters make up part of the available workforce pipeline if the wages are attractive enough to get them off the road.
- Have we adopted and embraced an industry-approved certification process that tells employers how many bronze, silver, gold, and platinum credentialed students are available in my community?
- Is there an active apprenticeship program for high school juniors and seniors with the region's manufacturing, retail, business, and industry bases?
- Is there a strong work-based learning program at my nearest community college supporting local business and industry with skilled workers?
- Are we being innovative in matching local education with the required skills of existing businesses/industries?
- What are my state and community competitors doing that we're not doing/what can I learn from their actions?
- What skills will be demanded of tomorrow's local workforce and can my community meet those demands? With appropriate credentials? Every good local economic development organization can answer this question through interaction with existing industries and matching the findings with high school curriculums.
- Am I an agent for education improvement or sitting on the sidelines? Are education improvement strategies part of the role of disruptive economic development? Am I engaging the right local education official for partnering opportunities? In many cases it will be the individual school principals because they are closest to the students and faculty and have a good handle on each school's situation. Lead, convene, or support!

America suffers a major skills gap, especially in the manufacturing sectors. It is no secret that global competition and innovations in technology are driving rapid changes in the U.S. economy. Much has been said over the years about the industrial employment shift in the mix and types of skills future American jobs will require. Many North American companies before, and especially after the Coronavirus pandemic, were considering reshoring, or moving business back to the U.S., Mexico, and to some degree Canada.

For a time, the U.S. flirted with the notion that we could more or less abandon manufacturing and become primarily a services economy. We have learned an important lesson: Manufacturing – our ability and willingness to make things – is vitally important to both the overall economy, jobs, and the diversity needed to maintain leadership in the U.S. It would be a sin to abandon such an integral part of who we are and the associated job base to chase sectors that may or may not survive in perpetuity, especially when the U.S. should lead the world in new technological manufacturing such as additive and smart processes.

The Future Jobs Education Requirements

There is a new reality for both workforce developers and education providers that a significant segment of today's labor force does not have the requisite skills demanded by employers. According to a study presented to the Business Council of Alabama by the Public Affairs Research Council of Alabama[79], in 1973 a third of all jobs could be filled by high school dropouts. The study projected that by 2020, those type jobs would have shrunk to just 12%. For jobs that could be filled with just a high school diploma, it was 40% in 1973 but expected to be only 24% by 2020.

---

79 Public Affairs Research Council of Alabama study for the Business Education Alliance, presented to the Business Council of Alabama, Aug. 17, 2016.

And, for jobs requiring postsecondary education and training, 28% required those credentials in 1973. When this book was ready for publication in 2020, 65% of jobs will require postsecondary training. (The training degrees or certificates include two-year colleges, trade schools, and four-year universities.)

The phrase "skills gap" is used in the public arena very loosely with varying understanding of what a "gap" in "skills" actually means. According to ACT's *"A Better Measure of Skills Gap,"*[80] a skills gap measures the difference between the skills needed for a job versus those skills possessed by a prospective worker(s).

For our purposes, accepting that your community probably has skill gaps, especially considering your targeted industries, is paramount for success in the recruiting process. Failure to admit the gap exists, address the gap, and improve the local talent pipeline will, quite often, ensure project elimination and, ultimately if it happens enough, community economic stagnation. Across the country, the economic "hot spots" have initiated efforts to improve K-12 education, adopt innovative methods to help older students identify work paths, and match the needs of employers with the required educational curriculum. State leaders are now talking about their populations achieving some form of certification past high school to be considered ready for employment in the advanced industries coming in the near future.[81]

I Have the Workforce for your Project. Really, Then Prove It!
Another way to state the challenge is "skill mismatch." One definition is that skill mismatch is used to describe a gap between the demand and supply sides of the labor market. According to ACT's *"A Better Measure of Skills Gap,"* many economists have used the term "skill mismatch" to describe patterns in structural unemployment,

---

80 https://www.act.org/content/dam/act/unsecured/documents/abettermeasure. pdf

81 Ibid

a situation in which jobs are available but cannot be filled due to a lack of necessary skills in the unemployed. The workforce possesses the wrong skills for the current industrial base, targeted industrial prospects, or both.

One of the discussion points today is the potential impact of innovation, technology, and artificial intelligence on future jobs' requirements. As one site consultant said, economic developers must be thinking and planning a decade ahead to be successful.

Alignment

The successful economic developer and community leader must address skill mismatches that exist within their domain to compete in the big league of economic and community development. Almost every study indicates that too often education curriculum and industry needs aren't aligned, allowing skill mismatches to occur.

Research has identified several key factors that contribute most to manufacturing with "*the most important factor being a nation's ability to foster talent-driven innovation. More specifically, "a key factor is our ability to ensure a sufficient supply of talented workers, which enables companies to advance innovation agendas and produce more innovative, higher-value goods and services capable of winning in global markets.*"[82]

One familiar saying is that if you're standing still, you're backing up. Disruptive economic development must evaluate and motivate at the local level to improve the talent pipeline. Waiting on someone else will neither address the workforce competitiveness issue that every vibrant community should address nor help a community win in the recruitment and expansion competition.

Across the country, the number of high school students taking trade or industry-related vocational/technical courses in prep for a

---

82   *Help Wanted, American Manufacturing Competitiveness and the Looming Skills Gap*, Deloitte University Press, Issue 16, 2015, page 98. https://www2.deloitte.com/content/dam/insights/us/articles/manufacturing-skills-gap-america/DR16_help_wanted.pdf

skilled or craft labor job has declined significantly in the past decade – in some states a decline of more than 40 percent. Too few students see craft/skilled labor as a career option because it's often viewed as "second class." But, in reality, trade/manufacturing jobs requiring an advanced training certificate not only pay very competitive wages but also require candidates who are smart and talented.

> Deloitte Consulting has reported that more than 70 percent of human resource executives indicate that incoming workers with inadequate skills is their most serious problem. The study also indicated that six out of ten open skilled production positions are unfilled due to talent shortage even when 80% of manufacturers are willing to pay more than market rates.
>
> And, it's going to get more difficult. Almost three million manufacturing employees in 2015 were 55 years of age or older and, in normal circumstances, likely to leave the labor force over the next decade. However, recessionary pressures that began around 2008 postponed retirement for some older workers, but it just delayed the inevitable. The looming talent shortage of both experienced workers and a new skilled workforce is affecting manufacturing companies' ability to meet growing customer demand.
>
> Deloitte's Skill Gap Study estimates that 3.4 million manufacturing jobs are likely to be needed by 2025 but only about 1.4 million are likely to be filled. That means two million jobs unfilled due to the skills gap.[83]

In today's competitive world, the simple local statement "we can provide the required workforce" for a project is not enough. As one site consultant said, "We're going to ask you to prove it."

---

83 Ibid. Page 100.

Hartley Powell, retired site selection executive with KPMG says that "most communities do not or cannot substantiate the quantity and quality of their workforce!" He continues that most RFP talent responses from communities in his long career were:

- Number of graduates
- Listing of schools
- Population Counts/Numbers
- Industry meetings
- Pre-employment programs

Mr. Powell says that communities must learn to prove their workforce for a specific project by "a preponderance of evidence."[84] In a paraphrased version of Merriam Dictionary's definition of "preponderance of evidence," it is essentially the standard of proof in which the community stating the fact *must* present evidence that is more credible, convincing, and shows that the fact to be proven is more probable than not.

The answer to whether a community has the necessary talent hinges on specific data evidence and alignment between education and local industry. Measurement is a key to continued progress and the most competitive economic development agencies rely on sophisticated data to present their case to the prospect or to a local company that is looking to expand.

As communities adopt aligning education and workplace goals, certification, and credentials processes, they help employers save time and money by quickly pinpointing individuals who have the essential, certified workplace skills. This alignment and linkage are designed to measure and close the skills gap – and build common frameworks that link, align, and match a community's workforce efforts. Remember, the skills gap measures the difference

---

84 Hartley Powell Teaching Session, Advanced Economic Development Leadership Program class, November 2019

between the skills needed for a job vs. skills possessed by a prospective worker. Effectively addressing gaps in the workforce helps grow the local talent pipeline.

Disruptive economic development and community leadership help ensure that a community is prepared at all levels to compete for higher-paying, quality jobs. Today's job creation currency is talent so, rather than sitting on the sidelines hoping for improvement, the change agent will begin formulating a plan to work inside the community with key partners and stakeholders to address the talent challenge.

Long gone are the days of wining and dining to win job creation projects. Effective use of workforce data and a preponderance of evidence are now accepted standards for the professional economic development agency. The most detailed evidence is essential:

- Technology school/community college support in the region.
- Description of the K-12 curriculum programming focusing on the segments important to the prospect and the local employers, e.g. computer coding.
- Graduation and dropout rates. Data to show how local and regional education is improving and dropout rates are decreasing.
- Test scores from 8th-grade math and reading – where do you rank vs. state and the U.S.?
- Percentage of students with an ACT silver credential rating or higher?
- Number of specialists that have graduated from tech schools, community colleges, and local universities in the last three years, i.e., welders, engineers.
- Ability to respond to SIC and NAICS code requests with accurate, understandable data and information.

- Industry-specific high school academies especially those that relate to a community's targeted prospects and existing companies.
- A listing of apprentice programs and internships with numbers.
- Commuter corridors and patterns – examples from existing companies – especially the percentage of the local population commuting elsewhere for work? (In most cases, these are your potential local workforce for projects looking inside your community – those commuting outside your community are like good debt!)

The World Is Flat

The New York Times Thomas Friedman correctly wrote that the world is flat. America's economic competition is not just the state next door but emerging manufacturing powerhouses across the globe. Just look at the manufacturing influx to Mexico and the issue it became in the 2016 presidential election. Approximately $1.4 billion in trade each day crosses the U.S./Mexico border with millions of jobs created on each side. Mexico is the second-largest trading partner to the United States, and approximately six million jobs in the U.S. depend on trade with Mexico.

America's trade pacts have become a giant political football with little recognition of how much impact global trade has on the U.S. and foreign economies until Covid-19 got everyone's attention.

The world is undergoing a new manufacturing order driven by economic, consumer, technological, market, and geopolitical forces with other countries well-positioned to take advantage of this new global landscape. In 2018, as auto consumer demands were dramatically changing, love for SUV/truck models rose dramatically and electric vehicle production was increasing, GM announced major plant closures and employment reductions to adapt to changing demands.

Northeastern University president Joseph Aoun's book *Robot-Proof*[85] challenges U.S. higher education to adapt its curriculum to better prepare students for the rapidly changing work environment. He says, "The only certainty about the future is change."

"Driverless cars are hitting the road, powered by artificial intelligence. Robots can climb stairs, open doors, win Jeopardy, analyze stocks, work in factories, find parking spaces, and advise oncologists. In the past, automation was considered a threat to low-skilled labor. Now, many high-skilled functions, including interpreting medical images, doing legal research, and analyzing data are within the skill sets of machines," says Dr. Aoun.

He states, however, that "...the dawn of the robot age **will be an opportunity**, not a threat." He argues that a "robot-proof" education is not concerned solely with topping up student's minds with high-octane facts. Rather, it calibrates them with a creative mindset and the mental elasticity to invent, discover, or create something valuable to society."[86]

Studies show that many of our international counterparts are providing a better education to students than are we. Among advanced nations, American students place anywhere from the middle to the bottom of the pack in all three continuing comparative studies of achievement in math, science, and general literacy.

---

85   Robert Aoun, *Robot-Proof: Higher Education in the Age of Artificial Intelligence*, MIT Press, August 2017
86   Ibid.

As we move toward the next decade, the U.S. places 17th in the developed world for education excellence according to a Pew Research study, *The Learning Curve*[87]. Finland, South Korea, Hong Kong, Japan, and Singapore sit in the top five with definite reasons for education success:

- Education is highly valued in these countries,
- Parents have high expectations for both teachers and students,
- **Parents are very involved in their children's education**, and
- Both educators and parents demand accountability for performance.

America competes on the global stage but, at present, we are not preparing students on a global standard that is rigorous and demanding – too much political correctness circulating in debates when our communities, states, and nation should be focused on world-class education and taking the rigorous steps to achieve that goal.

And, as Dr. Aoun challenges, education must prepare students to create, invent, and discover rather than absorb facts. Albert Einstein echoed the same principle "...education is not the learning of facts but the training of the mind to think."[88]

In each community, the local economic developer can be a change agent to help his/her community as they reinvent education to meet the evolving needs of manufacturing and business. As Jim Collins advised in his book *Good to Great*, you have to "get the right people

---

87 *The Learning Curve* / The Pew Charitable Trusts, April 13, 2020

88 Quoted in *"Einstein: His Life and Times"*, by Philipp Frank, published by Alfred A. Knopf, New York, 1947.

on the bus and in the right seats"[89] for the community to achieve economic success. Then to quote Mia Hamm, the U.S. Women's Soccer star, "Celebrate what you've accomplished, but raise the bar a little higher each time you succeed."[90]

---

89 Jim Collins, *Good to Great: Why Some Companies Make the Leap and Others Don't*, Harper Collins, October 16, 2001.

90 Mia Hamm, Aaron Heifetz (2013). *"Go For The Goal: A Champion's Guide To Winning In Soccer And Life"*, p.23, Harper Collins

CHAPTER 11

TRAINING THE MIND TO THINK

David first attended economic development training in his second year in the profession. One of the state universities offered an introductory basic course that featured speakers from the state economic development organization, utilities, local seasoned practitioners, and academia. While it inoculated David, it didn't fully explore the principles necessary to grow in the profession.

In his fifth year, David began his certification process and completed the course work and testing to earn his CEcD credential. Now almost ten years into his economic development career, David sought a deeper dive into the profession and found a new program initiated by five major universities.

The experiential program opened new learning doors and challenged long-held beliefs about the role of professional economic developers. He also met and interacted with professionals from across the country and began networking long after the program to gain from their successes and failures.

Training became a central strategy in the Bedford EDA as specialized learning programs were established for elected officials and members of the organization's advisory board. As elected officials completed the training programs, David and his staff noticed that they were more engaged during project presentations and certainly more informed as incentive, property, and abatement decisions came before the group.

David had always valued thought diversity within his staff and, based on some of the training sessions, more clearly understood the necessity of having varied opinions and ideas within his team. He realized that diversity challenged people's thinking and forced each one to better prepare for discussion and project competition.

The broad training for staff, elected officials, and board members was having an impact on the team's ability to prepare for Project Penguin – in a good way. It was also impacting the critical discussions about how to move Bedford beyond the pandemic. David and Betsy were reaching out to colleagues they met during advanced training, getting their ideas on recovery. Everyone was willing to share because everyone felt each other's pain.

Albert Einstein wrote that "...education is not the learning of facts but the training of the mind to think."[91] Professional economic developers have several training options from the basic to the advanced.

Established in 1962, Oklahoma University's Economic Development Institute provides its professional training program through on-line courses and traditional in-person institute settings. IEDC's certification program offers the most recognizable credential, the Certified Economic Developer (CEcD). IEDC has

---

91 Quoted in *"Einstein: His Life and Times"*, by Philipp Frank, published by Alfred A. Knopf, New York, 1947.

developed a process to prepare professionals to take the CEcD exam after candidates meet experience and professional development criteria. Training courses that lead to the exam are all IEDC Training Courses including six courses from OU EDI and the accredited basic economic development courses available at approved universities.

Five major universities – The University of Alabama, Clemson University, the University of Southern Mississippi, Texas Christian University, and the University of New Mexico — created the newest program, the Advanced Economic Development Leadership (AEDL) executive education program. The AEDL targets mid and senior-level economic development professionals and prefers at least five years' full-time experience and a basic certification to qualify for the program.

Today's professional economic developer must stay abreast of trends, challenges, and issues in evolving job creation strategies and, finding the perfect training curriculum, faculty, and approach is essential. The learning approach varies among the established programs and reviewing the curriculum/faculty can offer basic guidance for the interested professional.

With the CEcD the most recognized credential, the IEDC program attracts practitioners who want to learn but also desire that designation next to their name. Some economic development organizations state that the designation is preferred when job searches are conducted. The CEcD designation is also coveted in Canada and other countries.

The AEDL is designed to be a deep dive into contemporary economic and community development subjects. This experiential course focuses on a curriculum that deviates from the traditional programs to examine, explore, debate, and discuss issues and challenges in the ever-evolving world of economic development. This is why AEDL program participants are limited to experienced practitioners.

Whether basic or advanced, the principle remains the same – professional training is an important part of the practitioner's professional development. Given today's rapid pace of change, direct reports needing to act more independently, and the need to stay current to remain competitive, training EDO executives is a must.

CHAPTER 12

LOVING YOUR
EXISTING INDUSTRIES

Harry Walker ran one of Bedford's oldest businesses that designed and assembled boats for the highly competitive leisure recreation industry. It had rankled him for years the local companies were an afterthought versus attracting the new industry into town. Several employers had closed recently and the feeling among the existing business base was that the community just wasn't doing enough to support the companies that were already there.

Finally, enough was enough. He had invited David and Betsy to come out to his facility for a sit-down discussion about the importance of his business to the community and many others who were the lifeblood of the local economy.

When David and Betsy left the plant, it was clear that the EDA had not given local existing businesses the attention they needed. Driving back to the office they talked non-stop about what could be done to support and potentially mine the rich field of local companies.

Now those conversations with several local businesses were coming back to life as the pandemic impacted so many lives and pocketbooks. David and the chamber president sat down for discussions about their roles in recovery and also how they might better support the community's existing companies and small businesses in these uncertain times.

In the past, the chamber had hosted a luncheon during the State's annual Manufacturing Week. Beyond rubber chicken and some plaques, they had not done much to support the local base. And, the EDA had done even less because, in their minds, it fell into the chamber's backyard. Clearly, things had to change, had to change now, and in an impactful way.

David was being bombarded with articles and webinars about how important the existing base was to a recovering community. In their initial visit to the manufacturing facility, Harry Walker had laid the groundwork and explained to him in real terms that the EDA needed to take a more aggressive role with the home folks and, quite honestly, it could actually impact in a good way his recruiting efforts. Important data about suppliers and customers was there for the taking. It was like leaving money on the table.

Betsy from the EDA and John Hankins from the chamber formed a two-person SWAT team formulating a strategy that its action steps could be shared and implemented by the EDA, chamber, local governments, and the business community leaders. They looked at four other comparable cities that had faced similar challenges but had developed programs that not only helped sustain but grew the existing base. Now they were reaching out again just to see if their colleagues had any new brilliant recovery ideas.

The aggressive existing base program they rolled out last year was now being updated as a result of the pandemic. In their initial plan they had uncovered regulatory issues that impeded growth and, in partnership with local governments, solved many of the burdensome rules. They were a bit ahead of the pandemic recovery phase because the partnership was in place and many of the intangible walls had come down.

In the original plan, the chamber and EDA jointly launched a series of specific sector activities like Tech Thursdays and Aerospace Tuesdays where like industries sat down to discuss common problems and formulate possible solutions. It was not long before new relationships developed among attendees, new business ideas emerged, and the chamber/EDA leaders better understood the needs of key existing sectors.

As a side benefit, they discovered some partner industries for the school's apprentice program and were able to implement a communications plan focused on tenth-grade, eleventh-grade, and senior students with the message that making things was cool and a good paycheck was really cool.

Harry Walker joined the EDA board a year ago and is on a path to move into the leadership queue.

Eighty percent of a community's growth is from within. The tendency, however, is to focus on the sexy aspect of economic development: recruiting or attracting new companies or industries.

Today's successful economic developers work their existing industries constantly to understand the issues/challenges facing the local facility and home companies; show how much they are valued; and mine them for valuable information about suppliers, prospects, customers, and growth opportunities. In a time of transition and renewed emphasis on existing businesses, good information about the home office and local plants will provide more time to take advantage of what intelligence is gained. Where do local facilities rank among their sister plants on cost, output, and growth potential? Are local facilities keeping up with sister plants and their competition on owner investment to stay up to date on the latest production methods and equipment? Product and production changes usually mean new investments. If a local facility is not updating in a changing world, a cause for concern may be required.

In addition to being a great local employer, many of these community partners can play a vital role in the recruiting process. Quite often, a prospective company wants to meet with several of the community's existing industries to learn first-hand about workforce, community, and leadership experiences. They want an honest answer to what it's like being part of the community. It may be the local CEO or HR person, but their candid comments to the prospect can potentially make or break a project.

In fact, the relationship with the existing business sector can go a long way toward testimonials that influence a prospect toward the community, not away from the community. There is a well-known horror story that an existing industry HR director candidly told the prospect privately "You really don't want to move to this community" and proceeded to outline the reasons why. If the local economic developer was doing his/her job with the existing industry base, that unfortunate situation should not happen. Remember, the best surprise is no surprise. Building and maintaining strong relationships with existing industries will go a long way toward supportive local partners.

Often, EDOs have formal existing industry programs that garner spotted results. The key for success is to develop a program that is results-based rather than activity-based. Sure, it looks good to your EDA leadership to have positive reports of local visits, but it is much more effective to have a program that focuses on the needs of the existing industry community and what you are doing to help and the outcomes you achieve.

The best way to engage existing industries is face to face in either small group sessions or individually. Some EDOs hold small informal meetings to interact, identify emerging issues, and build bridges to local businesses. Often the session will include government officials or other community leaders to participate in these healthy discussions. One agency labeled the monthly sessions "8 at 8" – eight leaders around the table at 8:00 a.m. for strong coffee, pastries, fruit, and candid discussions.

Other communities hold industry-specific meetings to focus on issues related to their world. For example, in strong automotive areas, the EDO holds meetings with the automotive-related companies to ensure that key issues are aired, best practices shared, and networks strengthened. This approach can be replicated for other key industry sectors. A word of caution: once you begin such a program, meet consistently, keep the meetings informative, relevant, and **always follow through** and report on issues that require action.

As communities diversify culturally, it is important to focus on ways to integrate various international companies into the community. While there are nuances within various company environments, all can learn from each other if given the right platform and encouragement. Business approaches are often different within various cultures but the same objective exists; **operate a profitable company in a business-friendly environment with a trained, dependable workforce**. The EDO can serve the role of facilitator among all existing industries and break down barriers that might create walls and impede success.

An Action Plan

Every organization with the economic development function should have a working strategy to meet with their key existing companies at least once a year and the meeting should follow a process which will also accomplish several objectives:

- Select the key companies in your community that are influencers with a strong impact on the local economy – always include your business and industry investors.

- Send a personal letter requesting an appointment to the most senior company person but copying the gatekeeper
- Within a week of the letter reach out to the company – either to the senior executive or gatekeeper to personally request an appointment
- Be prepared to answer questions regarding the purpose of the meeting or have talking points ready to use as part of the meeting request. The meeting purpose should focus on their needs, not yours. In other words, we want to discuss any issues that may be adversely affecting their business, assist in solving them, outline strategies to make them more successful, and thank the business for its impact on the community.
- After three unsuccessful attempts to set the meeting, drop the effort, and move on.
- Once the meeting is set, confirm via email with a short purpose and who will be attending from the EDA team – no more than two or three with each participant having a role in the meeting.
- Send a reminder one week before the appointment – "looking forward…"
- Study the company's background and local situation before the appointment – always go prepared to the meeting with a series of "toss-up" questions that are designed to ensure discussion and break the ice. **Do your homework** – it will help avoid dumb questions that indicate you haven't taken the time to get to know their business.
- Put the person(s) at ease – stress the confidentiality of all information unless agreed otherwise or as part of an action item with outside agencies.
- Anticipate 45 minutes to one hour per discussion and **always include a company/plant tour**. Most companies love to show off what they do. Pay close attention and observe.

You can learn so much about a business by using your eyes and ears.

- Notice and note in your company working profile any personal items in the office that can be used in follow up communications, i.e., number of children, school-age, alma mater, sports interests, etc. An effort to personalize future communications will be warmly received.
- Also, keep tabs on media relating to the company which can be used in future meetings or communications – sometimes there is intelligence that can provide insight into company plans, products, and possible changes.
- Within a couple of days after the interview, send an email or snail mail letter of appreciation for the meeting, and recap any action items that were agreed upon. Even better: send a hand-written personal note.
- **A MUST**: Follow through on action items and report back to the company with findings. This is an essential follow up step that will reinforce the genuineness of the meeting and your intent.
- Repeat the process at least annually – keep detailed notes and files to help prepare for future visits. In most cases, you should begin to receive personal interaction from the people with whom you build relationships. They will see you as a problem solver.
- Have someone in the EDO that has responsibility for managing this function as a part of their job description. Remember, the success of your existing business is part of the gravity that improves your ability to attract new business.

This section comes with a **warning label**: If you are not serious about this process, don't attempt it. Mishandled, it can do more harm than good. However, if you are serious about working key existing companies, the process can pay huge dividends in relationships, networks, prospect data, and potential new investor revenue for the EDO.

In a results-based existing industry program, the banquet honoring local industries can co-exist with the efforts to interact individually or in small groups. The objective is to communicate to the community's existing business foundation that they are vitally important to the growth of the community.

CHAPTER 13

OUTSIDE THE INTERSTATES

If you don't know whose signs these are, you
can't have driven very far
—Burma-Shave sign

Get Your Kicks on Route 66
—Robert "Bobby" Troup: Actor, Composer, Pianist, Singer

Three of the four EDA staff hailed from fairly small or medium-size communities, so the challenges facing Bedford were somewhat familiar. The closest interstate was about ten miles to the south, so distance presented marketing challenges and opportunities. The state's longest river traversed only eight miles from downtown and the passenger train that used to have stops daily now only echoed the sounds of the locomotive barreling through town.

At the recent state-level economic developers' annual conference, the continuing debate about incentives and programs specifically for the more rural areas raged with no resolution in sight. Few understood the need for an economic vibrancy that touched the entire state and the impact striving communities would have toward a thriving state. Too often, those in charge saw job creation through blinders that mainly focused on the interstates.

David often returned to his hometown of eight thousand souls to visit his remaining family. Almost every time he ventured downtown he reflected on the way things were while growing up, and how little life had changed in the ensuing years. It was frustrating but revealing of what used to be – it was a snapshot of what was and was not happening in too many similar communities across the state.

On a recent trip to the state's capital city, he and the Secretary of Commerce shared these concerns over Clara's famous fried chicken. The answers were elusive but both agreed that more effort was needed in the heartland of the state. Out of the meeting came the concept of a special task force to present solid recommendations to the Governor on ways to strengthen communities off the interstate. Now with the pandemic recovery sweeping the nation, countless rural communities were struggling to find some normalcy and there would be many more meetings, recommendations, and actions before a light appeared at the end of the tunnel.

U.S. Route 66 first saw traffic in 1926 and for years was the most famous pathway in America, traversing nine states and 2,448 miles. Business owners enjoyed prosperous times during a forty-year stretch as people traveled from Chicago to Los Angeles and all points in between. Just as America's rural areas have experienced a decline, so did the famous highway when the national interstate system was built teasing drivers to travel unimpeded over those many hundreds of miles.

And when they did travel the famous route in its hey-day, chances were they would see the Burma-Shave signs that became a sensation during the same period. Mostly on rural roads, the six or seven signs in a row drove sales to record heights, but as the interstate system took over, Burma Shave suffered at the cash register.

While Route 66 (and Burma Shave) are nostalgic for many and an adventure for others, the route, in its entirety, no longer exists. A few stretches resurrect the joys of dreamers but the financial glory days are long gone.

So it is for many of America's rural areas.

So-called rural areas are suffering – some organic, some self-induced, and some just plain being ignored. But no matter the cause, many areas of the U.S. are hemorrhaging jobs and revenue.

We often forget why a community even exists. History plays a large role in establishing the purpose and ultimately the pride we feel towards our hometown. The key to survival and, hopefully, thriving is not to dwell in the past and not to try to be something unrealistic but to **embrace what makes a community unique and special**.

If we look at a community's evolution correctly and honestly, changes can serve a purpose to strengthen rather than weaken. "The very definition of change demands that it brings people and ideas together without coercion"[92] using the positive inertia to find a community's ...growth, or at least, sustaining sweet spot. A small team of committed and dedicated citizen leaders can make a huge difference in reviving a community, especially if they work to involve the entire community in the process. It may not be a complete restoration, but the revival can define a community's current value and establish pathways to reach realistic goals.

Community Gate Keepers

Many smaller communities have what's commonly called "Gate Keepers" – people whose families have lived in the community since its founding and they have made a good living. The

---

92 Michael Horton, *Top 10 Reasons Rural Community Development Is So Hard to Do*, The Center for Rural Affairs Newsletter, March 20, 2007. https://www.cfra.org/newsletter/1206.htm

community has been good to them and too often they don't want to see change, growth, and higher wages come in and disrupt the status quo and their golden balloon.[93]

But, the ripple effect from an expanding local economy just might mean increased dollars to spread around – more spending ability resulting from economic expansion and certainly more local tax revenue for government coffers - in essence, a larger pie from which to feast. Or it might, as they say on the golf course, stop the bleeding – maintain a reasonable community base.

Parochial attitudes often contribute to communities shutting themselves off from the outside. In this context, parochial means having a limited or narrow view of new ideas. This circling the wagons approach is not the way to revive a community's spark.

One young economic developer in an off the beaten path county stated a lesson that should be obvious but often isn't. She said, "I have accepted that this county cannot be something that its limited assets and geography won't let it be. We're not going to have success in the industry recruiting competition. So, my goal is to make the most out of what we have, accept it, and not try to make us something we'll never become."

Unrealistic goals can completely stifle the quest for successful community development because impossible goals tend to produce frustration through unrealistic expectations. Some communities are just not prepared or equipped for large-scale economic development or competing with their bigger neighbors. This does not mean they should completely give up but will require innovative thinking or, perhaps, building an entirely new box.

The road to effective community and economic development is long and hard. In some cases, the community must begin with the basics – overcoming distress rooted in illiteracy, teenage pregnancy, low high school graduation rates, drug use, crime, poor-performing schools, population losses, and inadequate health

---

93   Ibid.

care. Addressing deep systemic problems is usually the right first step but struggling communities are not usually inclined or funded adequately to make significant improvements. It's the proverbial chicken and the egg. The key is to get started. Our job in economic and community development is to make it easier for those wanting to make a positive difference.

While it is true that all politics is local, it is also true that economic development is local. In other words, local elected officials will be judged on what happens in their communities but also compared against what happens in the community next door or down the road. "Why didn't we get this or that and they did?"

As long as the community expresses some real competitive fire then there is enough local spirit left in the tank to make progress. It's when a community loses its heart and soul, becoming totally lethargic, that foretells a long dry spell.

It's Tougher in Small Town America

It's tough for small-town America to break into the competitive circle for job creation and a thriving economy. But just as the old, old saying about whining in baseball, there is no whining in economic development. In the end, each community is responsible for its own success or failure.

Some states provide special programs for "rural" areas to increase their competitiveness. But in reality, successful job creation at the local level begins with an approach that reflects the character and assets of the community. The trick is to identify the strengths that will resonate with targeted prospects, existing businesses, and entrepreneurs.

Quite often, small-town America is made up of simple, family-oriented communities with strong "connections" among citizens, groups, and institutions. The right prospects must see that there is pride in the community which will naturally translate into pride in their work, and the company they work for as well. The key is to match specific economic and community development strategies to companies who value the assets/resources embedded in America's heartland.

But just as important is to employ a strategy that focuses on the broad definition of job creation by supporting existing industries, establishing a pathway for entrepreneurs, and encouraging small business development. According to the Small Business Administration Office of Advocacy, small businesses represent 99.7 percent of all employer firms. Since 2005, small businesses have generated 64 percent of U.S. new jobs and paid forty-three percent of the total private payroll.[94]

There is no magic bullet for success in Middle America for project attraction. Site consultants, company decision-makers, and state development agency project managers usually go toward low hanging fruit and familiarity, i.e., along the interstates and in the urban areas. However, many communities are expanding their focus to the broad definition of economic and community development – commercial, entrepreneurial, retail, tourism, and building a strong existing industry program. Together, these sectors may produce job creation results beyond the typical buffalo hunt.

Some experts contend that declining population rural areas without infrastructure assets should forego traditional recruitment and focus on community development and the other pathways toward job creation. With the elected official's mindset, this may be a bridge too far for some communities, but it is worth an honest conversation. However, with such a discussion, the professional economic developer needs to have strategies to recommend or already in place to create and/or maintain jobs sans recruitment.

---

94 Source: U.S. Census Bureau, SUSB, CPS; International Trade Administration; Bureau of Labor Statistics, BED; Advocacy-funded research, Small Business GDP: Update 20022010, www.sba.gov/advocacy/7540/42371. Source: https://www.sba.gov/sites/default/files/FAQ_Sept_2012.pdf

Some Lessons

- Identify your unique community character – can the essence of the community be bottled and sold? Will decision-makers buy what you are selling?
- Identifying community strengths can often be harder than identifying weaknesses. To almost everyone, the weaknesses are apparent but not so much the strengths. Most communities are better than they think they are but not where they need to be in terms of economic vitality. Make sure to focus on the strengths too, especially as they relate to what you target businesses want!
- Who are your key internal players? When this or that person speaks, will most of the community listen? And, are they "bought into" a process and strategy? Again, think of a football team. If the team hasn't bought into the coaches' process and strategy, it will be a long season.
- Who are outside advocates from your community? Who will speak up for your community at the State Capitol or in the boardroom?
- Can you take negatives and turn them into positives?
- Can you find a role in retooling your community for anyone that desires a role? Bringing a community back to life should be shared among the entire citizenry. Shared Issues + Shared Opportunities + Shared Resources = Shared Results.
- Can you work across city and county lines to gain mutual benefit? Is this an opportunity to band together with another county and join forces to jointly grow the region? Can both the figurative and literal walls come down to find common marketing ground? (See section on Realities of Alliances)
- What is your community's charm factor? What will outsiders find appealing about your community? Matching charms with the right companies do not just happen – it requires a lot of matchmaking and sweat equity.

- "Just Do It!" Nike nails it. Quit sitting around complaining or talking about it – Just Do It! There's no whining in economic development.[95]

---

[95] Once you have compiled your information, consider using outside resources. Every College of Business teaches Marketing and Strategic Planning courses at the undergraduate level. Some have graduate level courses. Many perform projects for outside companies and public organizations. The University of Southern Mississippi College of Business and Economic Development has a Masters in Economic Development program which meets primarily online. All of the working professional student's projects can be focused on the community they come from.

CHAPTER 14

MARKETING WITH A **TWIST**

When David took over the EDA, he did a deep dive look at the agency's operations, the community, and where the economic development program could realistically focus. He was a student of the Process approach and began the incremental steps that could lead to a competitive and vibrant community.

One area with obvious gaps was the agency's marketing efforts. No one had done a complete review of the program in years, and current efforts were spotty at best, not based on a well-crafted strategy.

David had worked with the Vision Clear marketing firm in his past life and decided to call them in for a review. The world of place branding and marketing had changed dramatically over the past decade and, if Bedford wanted to compete, it needed to evolve as well.

After a month of evaluation which included focus groups and a review of current marketing efforts, the firm was ready to present its findings and recommendations. The initial session would involve the staff only for reaction and then adjustments would be made as they tweaked and readied it for prime time.

David and his staff were taking a measured approach to developing an agency strategic action plan, with each team member assigned one key area to shepherd. The marketing and strategic plans had to be based on community realities but also present an aspirational appeal.

Of course, all these continuing efforts were sandwiched in with Project Penguin and the pandemic recovery efforts, both of which now consumed the agency's full attention. The marketing approach of several months ago would dramatically change if they won Project Penguin and survived the pandemic economic recovery.

O h my! Do we market differently than the 1950s Burma Shave and Route 66 approach – we actually market differently than we did five years ago – maybe five days ago!

Marketing options are changing constantly and the audience's receptivity changes on a whim. Just look at television. In 1965, *The Andy Griffith Show* was the nation's number one television program. Can you even name one top show today, especially with hundreds of TV channels available with almost anything to view?

One year after the iPhone was introduced in 2007, Apple launched the App Store. After phenomenal growth over the past few years, global mobile app revenue is forecast for 2020 to be $189 billion. Apps and social media have totally revolutionized the way we communicate and market.

The national elections of 2016 demonstrated that old ways of communicating have gone out the window as social media grows toward becoming the most dominant source of information. A 2016 Pew Research Center study found:

- Driven by older consumers television news consumption was still dominant (57% TV to 38% Social Media) – Older consumers preferred TV (65 & older 85%; 50 – 64 72%).

- Online News was moving up driven by younger consumers – (50% of those aged 18 – 29 went online for news as did 49% of those aged 30 – 49).
- Radio news appealed to about 20% of adults. Print newspapers as a source for news had declined to 20% of adults.
- Print was mainly attracting the older crowd with 48% of those 65 and over reading a newspaper.[96]

So, translating an effective community marketing effort through all the clutter is not easy. It is, however, a necessary ingredient in a successful strategic plan.

Melissa Medley, beloved friend and until her passing, chief marketing officer for VisionFirst Advisors, recognized that almost every EDO has a strategic plan, but not all have a strategic marketing plan. "A plan helps you focus on what's most important and say 'no' to those things which are not." She continued "Marketing is a process not a campaign."[97]

Today's successful marketing and political campaigns are rifle shots. They are directed at well-researched **specific targets** with snackable messages. If you are looking on a website for a hotel room at a particular brand, the next time you go to the CNN or MSNBC website for news updates, up will pop an ad for that particular hotel brand and often in the city in which you were searching for a room. Never underestimate that Big Brother is watching.

So, translate this into economic development targeted marketing. Gone are the days of mass mailings to an entire industry sector. **Today, a specific message should be sent to a specific group with a specific targeted message.** Site consultants say

96 *Pathway to the News*, Amy Mitchell, Jeffrey Gottfried, Michael Barthel and Elisa Shearer, % of U.S. adults who often get news from each platform, Pew Research Center, July 7, 2016 https://www.journalism.org/2016/07/07/pathways-to-news/

97 Melissa Medley Teaching Session, Advanced Economic Development Leadership Program class, November 2015.

over and over again that they want, even need, to hear what separates one community from the others. Solid, relevant, up-to-date information helps sort through the potential sites for project selection.

It is research and more research – specific data that identifies and then tailors the message to the prospect's decision-maker. And, differentiating my community from the others – why am I special to your company? How do we meet your needs? Answering these questions requires understanding your customer targets so that there is a better chance the message resonates. Then ask what message vehicles are working, which messages are penetrating, so your ability to influence decision-makers increases. Ask them, don't assume you know, even if you do. Eventually you find out that customers, even in the same business, look at their business differently as well as alike. Your ability to influence people increases when you know both.

Moneyball Economic Development
A favorite movie for baseball aficionados (maybe not purists) is "Moneyball." For the uninitiated, "Moneyball" is the story of the Oakland A's and General Manager Billy Beane's strategy to turn the A's into a winning team despite the smallest total team salary in major league baseball. After the last game of the 2001 season, Billy Beane (played in the movie by Brad Pitt) convenes a meeting of his scouts explaining on a board, "Here are the rich teams, then here are the poor teams, then there is fifty feet of crap and here we are."[98]

While other teams were concentrating on the traditional selection process for players i.e. batting average, home runs, and RBIs, Beane started looking at data, especially on-base percentages. He believed

---

98 Michael Lewis, *Moneyball: The Art of Winning an Unfair Game*, W.W. Norton & Co. March 17, 2003; Movie: *Moneyball*, Director Bennett Miller, screenplay by Stan Chervin with Steven Zaillian and Aaron Sorkin, Columbia Pictures, September 2011.

wins could be built on the quantitative data a player builds, not on the qualitative insight the scouts talked about. It worked for the A's the next year with a 20-game winning streak and a modified, data-driven approach adopted now by most big-league baseball teams.

Whether it's workforce, marketing, or RFPs, data should be a major component in economic development, maybe even the foundation. And, as a professional economic developer who is not paying attention to data and statistics, you might not be doing your job to the level it should be done if your organization doesn't have someone exploring data on everything that matters to community development and job growth. But beyond paying attention, *understanding* what data means and how it can be used to promote a community is essential.

Unfortunately, economic developers spend a lot of time and resources scouting for the home run hitters – that project that brings in hundreds of jobs while too often ignoring the singles, doubles, and jobs that might be developed as a start-up in someone's garage or the expansion opportunity in the existing business down the street.

It's the singles and even the bunts that actually undergird our economy - those growing companies that always seem to get on base, with little help from the buffalo hunters. Remember, small businesses in America account for 99% of U.S. businesses. The job of the professional is to help move them from first to second base and eventually home. The frequency of small business singles and doubles eventually mean their runs count just as much as the grand slam recruited job.[99] Billy Beane's 2002 Oakland A's in "Moneyball" looked for players who could get on base and eventually score – not solely the home run hitters. They threw out the playbook on how to value players and, instead of time-honored stats like "batting average" and decisions on which players to draft based on scouts' recommendations, data-driven stats like "on-base percentage" became a major part of the decision process.

---

99 As we stated before, your community's business success acts like gravity, attracting attention, and actually increases your chance of hitting a grand slam.

Beane led the team to a first-place finish in the American League West in the 2002 season, including a 20-game winning streak that stood until 2017. From then on, statisticians and data supplemented the scouts in searching for talent and almost every baseball team adopted the formula including the Boston Red Sox who vanquished the Bambino curse in 2004 and won their first World Series in almost 100 years – plus three more (and counting) for good measure.

But, Let's Start at the Beginning
Marketing is one of those terms everyone thinks they understand. Most see marketing as the search for the right message(s) for the community to stand out from the competition. This in fact is part of what marketing does, at least at the advertising agency or internal marketing department. Marketing is also the job of the leader, executive team, and board of the economic development organization. These are the people who must choose how to position the community toward a defined marketplace of prospects, consultants, allies, media, local businesses, and local community members. Getting everyone pulling on the rope in the same direction is marketing too.

The twist about marketing is always to do one thing especially well – **understand the people you want to influence first**, internal and external. You need to remember, the customer you are trying to influence has the final say. It is their decision to agree with you, locate or expand their business in your community, and/or do what you want to be done. People will not choose a location based on what you think is important. You must endeavor to know what they want to achieve. Then craft your message around those criteria and it will be more powerful.

You should, therefore, run everything you are learning about your community and the organizations you deal with through the question "What does this mean to the customer(s) I need to influence?" Remember, any advantage your community has only matters if a **customer values it**. Of course, customers can be taught to value community attributes, just remember to twist and understand their wants, needs, and desires first.

Following the twist approach, you get an additional benefit. Once you understand the people you want to influence, you now have the leverage you need to make your community story meaningful. You use the customer's terms, their concerns, their needs, everything that has a specific meaning to that particular customer in your presentation. This makes your message resonate and gives you the credibility needed to move them to the next step. From customer knowledge comes credibility, from credibility comes opportunity, and from opportunity comes success.

Here are some key marketing questions that should be answered before starting the marketing process and spending money:

- Is my community prepared for aggressive economic development and growth? Are there internal steps that need to be taken to get everyone aligned?
- Have we mined our local existing industries for supplier, vendor, customer, and other prospects?
- Are we content with singles and doubles or only interested in home runs? Have we convinced our elected and volunteer leadership the value of singles and doubles?
- When focused on attraction, have we identified and qualified industry sectors for targeting? Do we have the infrastructure and support mechanisms for the targeted sectors? Remember, not all industry sectors are practical for every location to recruit.
- Are we targeting both companies (especially growth companies) and site consultants? Ideally, EDAs are targeting both, recognizing that building a relationship with target companies before the company begins a formal site consultant relationship is an advantage. Of course, many communities wait until the RFP and respond. But a growing number of

aggressive communities are spending research time and dollars identifying and getting to company decision-makers before there is an active project and the formal process begins. If the company does decide to engage a site consultant, you want to be one of the first to know and begin networking with that firm. Remember, knowledge is power, and the Oakland A's devoted one key staff member before it was cool to do nothing but research/analyze players.[100] Also, recognize that 98% of American businesses have less than 20 employees and only 19,000 have 500 or more employees.

- Are the basics in place i.e. a first-class website with detailed information about the community with a special tab for site selectors and consultants as well as a simple process to contact the EDO staff? (Pet peeve: too many EDOs make it difficult or next to impossible to easily find contact information, especially email addresses.) Do local existing industries also have this key information?
- With the explosion of social media and apps, does your organization have an effective social media marketing strategy? Is it kept up-to-date and fresh? Note: Social media is not a one-way street. You are expected to participate in the "conversations." It is also an excellent way to communicate with your community.
- Are target industry sectors clear as well as the targets within sectors?
  - Name of firm/location
  - Key contact or decision-maker (LinkedIn?) and as much background on that person as possible to personalize and tailor the message – it's not enough to just know the name

---

100 Prospect lead generation companies exist and can economically improve your batting average. They can identify people interested in your location and/ or firms that are growing fast and may soon be looking for a new location.

of the company and send a shotgun blast. For success, it
must be personalized to the right company contact.

º   Types of products that match a community's assets.

º   Based on company research, how does your community
     compare to the prospect's existing' locations? Are there
     similarities that match well?

º   Are you requesting a meeting or just sending informa-
     tion? What is the purpose of the communication?

Traded and Non-Traded Companies

In *The New Geography of Jobs,* Enrico Moretti states that "While the
vast majority of jobs are in the non-traded sector, this sector is
not the driver of our prosperity. Instead, our prosperity mainly
depends on the traded sector." Moretti continues, "Although jobs
in local services constitute the vast majority of jobs, they are the
effect, not the cause of economic growth."[101]

In other words, car plants bring Walmarts, but Walmarts don't
bring car plants. Traded jobs (those we want to recruit and expand)
cause the creation of non-traded jobs and the resulting ripple
effect. For instance, an automotive assembly plant has the multiplier or ripple effect of about six to one. For every direct assembly
job, another six indirect and induced jobs are created in supplier
companies, professional jobs, service sector, and retail.

There are generally two types of companies looking for locations –
growing companies who are expanding their operations and companies wanting to relocate or consolidate.

In *Moneyball,* a baseball team dedicated a key person to do nothing but research potential players – to understand whether they
could get on base and score runs.[102] Communities must also invest

---

101   The New Geography of Jobs, Enrico Moretti, Houghton Mifflin, Boston
New York, 2012, Page 57.

102   Michael Lewis, *Moneyball: The Art of Winning an Unfair Game,* W.W. Norton
& Co. March 17, 2003; Movie: Moneyball, Director Bennett Miller, screenplay

in data and research to pinpoint companies that fit their needs, assets, and geography. In the end, a company might be a good fit for your community, but you also must be a good fit for them.

Branding/Marketing Intelligence

Your brand is a promise you make to a customer. It is a pledge the customer anticipates the community will keep based on the community's reputation, the customer's direct personal experience, and the experience shared by others. As such, brands are built on trust and credibility. Therefore, provide what you promise – a quality field visit, engaged city service providers, and/or visitor experience. You can't be the "friendliest bank in town" if the tellers are not happy to see customers when they walk up or drive through.[103]

Branding is the process of creating a unique image that differentiates your community in the customer's mind. A brand conveys the value promise given to your clients/prospects and how the community will live up to the promise. Done correctly branding is about getting to the stage where mentioning your name triggers a mental image of your promise.

Embedded in the above definition is one's reputation and ability to deliver. Place branding is an essential first step in economic development marketing but, for branding to be believable and successful, the community must understand its value proposition from the eye of the beholder as well as through their own eyes. If the community doesn't believe it, then it surely will be tough for the prospect to believe it.

Are the views of insiders and outsiders consistent? Are promises to prospects and existing businesses based on real-life or how we wish to be perceived? Both outside and existing company

---

by Stan Chervin with Steven Zaillian and Aaron Sorkin, Columbia Pictures, September 2011.

103 William C. Smith and Robert Ingram, *Building a Community Brand*, Economic Development Journal, Summer 2012, page 41-46.

decision-makers need to see that the brand marketed by a community is consistent with reality.

If you are trying to brand "Silicon Beach" when you have a beach but just a few technology companies and very little infrastructure to support the technology industry, you might fall flat when compared to very serious silicon cluster locations.

Site selection consultants view a lot of "good" communities with the mandate to whittle down the list to four or five finalists. Perception is reality for a major portion of the elimination process but when it gets down to the Final Few, perception and reality must mesh. To stay in the game, the marketing **message *and* reality must sync in the minds of the consultant and the prospective company.** Strategic communications can be one of the most powerful, most cost-effective tools that an economic development professional has in his/her arsenal – as long as it is targeted and based on fact. Note: Everybody isn't looking for the same thing, so make sure what your message says means something to the people you are hoping to connect with.

Engaging the Community
Place branding doesn't just happen. It can proceed over years and years of action and inaction. But in reality, places inherently have brands – some manufactured and some created organically. The increase in all types of media has led communities to be vulnerable to the images captured on social media and television. These images often shape the way the world and job creation prospects see a community.

Citizens are an integral part of building a community's brand and must be involved in the process to be successful. They have to believe it and invest their time and emotion as well. Otherwise, the brand becomes a community's tagline and not much more. It will be transparent to decision-makers whether a brand is real or not.

As an agent of economic development, engaging the community to work together in the goal of a shared vision is an essential local strategy. Within a community, key stakeholders should take ownership of the brand to ensure its credibility. And, as has been stated over and over again, it must be based on reality rather than perception. In other words, the brand needs to have deep roots within the community. Local stakeholders who will be making critical decisions on how they would like their community viewed include government, the private sector, education leaders, and the community as a whole.

A key benefit of a place branding strategy is to create a bridge between economic development strategies and community action. It is important that a community "buys-in" to the strategy to create new jobs and expand the existing business base. The citizens may not fully understand the strategy or the resulting payback but igniting a community's passion translates into an economic ripple effect throughout the region. When the leadership and citizens become passionate about their communities' direction, then a positive environment for economic growth can be spawned.

Therefore, it is important to flesh out a marketing/branding strategy that has tentacles and engages the community to support and take action. The strategy expands beyond an economic developer "just doing their work" to disrupting the environment in which the work is done. Such positive disruption can produce an opportunity to match community perception and reality. When the community as a whole understands who and what they are supporting and making choices for, it provides the elected officials and community leaders great cover for their tax or incentive investment in economic development. In most cases, such an approach requires out-of-the-box thinking on behalf of the professional economic developer.

The Taxi Driver

Site consultants and company reps should be able to sense the excitement in a community and, hopefully, a spirit of "oneness." When the taxi driver talks positively about the community and the café waitress gushes about how well her young daughter is doing in Mrs. Dees' fourth-grade class, the brand is organically reinforced.

In reality, place branding occurs with or without a strategy. Let's play word association. When you hear these names, what first comes to mind? Research Triangle, Florida, Silicon Valley, California, Portsmouth, Salt Lake City, Kansas City, Mississippi, Las Vegas, Binghamton, Chicago, Seattle, Birmingham, Atlanta, Nashville, and Dallas. Some of these brands have been created but some exist from years of national news stories and advertising. Everyplace has a brand, it has a name. Some are positive, some not so much. The question is, what are you doing with your brand?

Community brands are also more difficult to manage than product brands like Coca-Cola. Many people are involved in determining the experience the customer has when interacting with a community. Whereas a product brand can be sold in a retail outlet with poor customer service and still not get tainted from the bad experience, a community's brand can be tarnished just because one person was rude on the phone.[104]

Economic development professionals need the help of everyone who shares the vision of what makes your community/brand different. In most cases, you have to build this shared vision.

Brands are inherent therefore they must be managed through both creative, pinpoint marketing, and reality. According to Atlas Advertising[105], these are the traits that successful brands have:

- **Appearance** – How do they come across without saying a word?
- **Qualifications** – What they are good at – key assets that relate to your business interest?
- **Competencies** – Skills and services to help clients achieve their goals.
- **Achievements** - How has my community made an impact?

---

104 Ibid, page 42

105 Atlas Integrated, Economic Development Consultancy, Denver, Colorado. https://www.atlas-integrated.com/

- **Passions** – What do our citizens love about their community?
- **Value** – What can the community offer a prospect, site selector, and an employee?
- **Reputation** – How is our community viewed by others?
- **Personality** – A community's values, goals, identity, and behavior.
- **Differentiator** – Talents and traits that make us unique.

An Economic Development Organization SWOT

Just as a community needs a living, active strategic plan so does the economic development organization. The traits outlined above offer a good start for those who want to beef up their brand and engage the community in a unified strategy. Economic development agencies should lead in identifying the gaps between perception and reality so that an effective economic development marketing strategy can be developed.

A SWOT analysis is designed to tell you what you can accomplish given your resources and capabilities in a given environment with targeted customers.

ED Strengths

- What are the community and EDO doing right? Focus on the areas and positive stories that can be marketed to targeted prospects
- Who are your key local industries and employers? What are the stories you can tell about successes that resonate and translate to your prospects?
- What is making a difference in your marketing efforts – what is working? Are you asking questions and listening or talking and answering questions? More questions mean you are learning. Who has responsibility for analyzing website visits, conversations generated, etc.?

- Do we use local metrics creatively and wisely – measure what matters to decision-makers and present creatively through today's effective social and marketing mediums. Then analyze and decide on the best avenues for your message.
- What is the community value proposition to prospective business clients and existing companies?[106]

ED Weaknesses

- To this point, what hasn't or isn't working well? Why? Has it been corrected or updated?
- What hinders progress? Is it correctable or do we work around it?
- Are we being honest about areas that need attention to be more competitive? Quite often, site consultants and company decision-makers already know where the warts are – you can't sweep them under the rug.
- Is there a process to get honest feedback from those you are targeting?

ED Opportunities

- Almost every community has something(s) to market. What have we identified that is specifically marketable to certain industry sectors? This means matching your assets with the desires/needs of prospective companies. Show you've done the research to understand their business needs and how your community matches.
- What is a community or regional asset that we are not yet leveraging? Analysis, Analysis, Analysis.

---

106 The job is to provide value from the customer's perspective. To be successful, you need to understand the benefits the customer wants and the tradeoffs they are willing to make. Your customers value is based on what your offer does for them.

- Are you thinking five, ten years ahead? The pandemic will definitely change the way site selection is done and also the evolving sectors. How much reshoring will occur? Will it come from China or elsewhere? Are you a candidate? How well positioned are our existing industries within their sectors and their own companies? No better time than now to have those conversations.
- What changes in business models mean more opportunities for communities like yours? Who can help you understand these businesses better?

ED Threats

- Well, duh! The biggest one in decades has just knocked America in the mouth. How is it going to threaten communities beyond the obvious tax revenue loss, record high unemployment, shifting buying patterns, and probably reduced budgets for marketing? These and other threats are real!
- Who on the EDA staff is charged with tracking and analyzing adverse trends in the marketplace? Adverse trends include those impacting both your existing and potential businesses.
- Of all the times, the EDA staff should be visiting and communicating with stakeholders (which is discussed in detail in Chapter Four)
- Elections are always around the corner – will political changes impact the relationships between the EDA and governments?
- Negative perception of tools and information in the economic development marketing quiver – this threat or negative can be turned into a positive through constant analysis of what marketing tools are working/not working. Marketing dollars are precious!

Numerous studies have looked at place branding in the context of which brands and what approaches actually connect with the needs of prospective businesses. As almost every site selection consultant will caution, the selection process is one of elimination. Studies note that favorable images of places that fit the basic criteria are enhanced through branding that sears an image into the mind.

There is an old adage that there is no perfect site. The role of the site selector is to convince the client that a community is almost there and fits on most key areas. While the community may miss one or two criteria, it should be recommended for inclusion because of the key positive factors and strategies that address the deficiencies.

Bad or inaccurate branding can cause site selectors to perceive the community as a wrong fit or unsuitable place for their client to do business. Bad place branding can also provide an easy excuse to remove a community from consideration hence the critical need for accurate branding based on reality.

The Gaps

Numerous studies have highlighted the important criteria for site selection from both consultants and the local practitioners' perspectives. As effective marketers, it is essential to understand the important decision criteria and the gaps that may exist with each decision point and the local community.

For example, without question workforce and education rank high on every important criteria list. However, the locals' branding and marketing may state generally that "...we have a talented and well-trained workforce" but the site selector is looking much deeper at certain SIC or NAICS codes.

A simple, general statement will not get the job done. Today's selection decisions are based primarily on data, especially data to support a community's claims that they have a talented and well-trained workforce.

Branding meets reality surfaces in other criteria as well. Another area of strong agreement is a business-friendly local environment. One company representative said, "I want to go to a place that will get me to making money the fastest."

Efficient delivery of services is very important to decision-makers. If a community's branding touts "world-class permitting in 90 days or less," that is the benchmark. But, if the community's reputation through past experience says they cannot handle permitting within ninety days, count on being challenged and maybe not moving forward in the selection process.

Suffice it to say that perception and reality are important aspects of the selection process. Prospective companies must sort out reality in order to determine the final few sites for consideration. And the wise economic development team will look through the eyes of prospects to determine key areas that need community focus and attention.

International Marketing

Globalization has made cross-border business deals more commonplace than ever and communities sometimes face the issue of local team members jeopardizing projects by acting in an untoward way or just being unaware of other countries' customs, culture, or manners. Learning international protocol before meetings/events can have a great impact on how a community is perceived by the prospect. Several great books can simplify each country's basic cultural business issues so that even the rawest local team member can add to the experience – *Kiss, Bow or Shake Hands (Terri Morrison); Business Etiquette for Dummies (Sue Fox); and International Business Etiquette (Ann Marie Sabath).*

No-Nos range from cultural mistakes during business sessions to faux pas involving meals or receptions. Almost all are preventable with a little effort and homework. Learning the customs and culture of a foreign country demonstrates one's respect for an international prospect and is important to developing a strong business relationship that, hopefully, will continue when the company locates in the community.

Examples of foreign etiquette tips compiled from the three books mentioned earlier:

Japan   Hold a business card with both hands and silently read it carefully – don't write on it or shove it back into your pocket. Recognize that bowing is the appropriate greeting while offering a light handshake. Normally gifts are exchanged but avoid white wrapping paper and four is considered an unlucky number.

England   Keep your hands in sight rather than under the table or in your pockets. Hierarchy is important therefore, acknowledge the most senior person first. Yes, "Cheers" to signal for others to enjoy their beverages is good English etiquette when hosting a meal.

Mexico   The family is very important in Mexico. For that reason, it will be important to express interest in one's family during meals, visits, and follow up communication. They are also proud of their history and will be impressed if you make an effort to become acquainted with it. Many international faux pas are made regarding one's title or name. In Mexico, for a male, be sure to use their father's name when addressing them which will be the second last name you hear. (i.e. Pedro Gomez Rodriguez should be addressed as "Senor Rodriguez."

France   Never ask personal questions during a business meeting and remember that rank is important – begin with the highest level person. Give a lighter handshake that you might in the U.S. and wait for women to initiate a handshake. Always remain calm, polite, and courteous during business meetings.

Germany   They place a high value on both formality and professional titles. If a person is a doctor, professor, lawyer, or engineer, address the individual with the appropriate title followed by the last name (i.e. Herr Doktor Schmidt). Be on time for meetings – Germans expect

	punctuality. Wait to be invited into a room before entering. The pace of Germans making a decision is methodical – much slower than in the U.S. Emotional involvement is unacceptable in negotiations.
China	Be careful about chopsticks – the Chinese consider waving, pointing or vertically placing them on the rice bowl as extremely rude.
Singapore	Always give a gift to the company not to one person – to avoid the appearance of a bribe.

These are a few examples of cultural differences and customs that are important with international business sessions. And, it's not necessary to be in a foreign country for these and many others to apply. When an international company visits your community, many of the cultural nuances should be applied in an effort to impress the prospect that you have some understanding of their country.

It may be a good idea to hold a team meeting before traveling to a country or hosting an international visit just to be sure that everyone understands the basic formalities that are important. These small efforts with the local team will go a long way toward a fruitful and fun experience. Do your homework!

The Social World[107]

Site consultants prefer face to face interaction with economic developers but also recognize the role emails and social media have in effective communication. Websites are still the most common

---

107 Pay attention to research about audiences. The American consumer is part of the change we see. Customers make choices and things change. This recommendation is especially useful when it comes to social media. Did you know, as of 2019 social media usage in the U.S. was basically flat for the last four years, still significant, but flat. Then, of course, the pandemic changed that too. See a research report by Edison Research and Triton Digital titled, *The Infinite Dial 2019*, available for free at https://www.edisonresearch.com/the-social-habit-2019/

medium for communicating with consultants but do not take the place of face-to-face communication whenever possible. Websites are very useful for information on key criteria related to the beginning stage of a project, i.e., workforce/education data; cost of land, taxes, and fees; lifestyle indicators; sites/available buildings and regulations.

However, many site consultants find the information on community websites "lacking" which is unacceptable given the many templates and examples available to craft a website with information that is relevant and informative. An exciting, informative website is basic blocking and tackling. You've got to perfect this if you have any chance of effectively communicating.

Other mediums are gaining in importance to the marketing process. **Facebook** currently has about 1 billion users. **Twitter** has more than 320 million users and continues to grow as the debate about whether a U.S. president should communicate to the world in 280 characters. Twitter is an open network with the world as your audience. **Instagram** currently has 113+ million monthly active users and is a visual, artistic way to define and express your community.

A lot of social media is about experimentation – what works and what doesn't. That is why it's important to talk to your audience and understand for each client what works best. Social media is a combination of possible marketing tools which used properly can greatly expand a community's brand. But a successful social media strategy requires time, staff, and budget appropriate to the expected return on investment. Do not do social media as an "activity" based marketing effort – make sure the mediums selected bring the desired results and check those results often. Frequently, websites and materials are out of date and send a message that organizational professionalism is lacking.

Profiling, in a Good Way – Finding the Hook

Harvey Mackay[108] is a bestselling author, speaker, businessman, and expert on successful networking and marketing. He developed the *Mackay 66* customer profile in 1983 to help his Minnesota envelope company salespeople have critical information about their customers. He said that "armed with the right knowledge, you can outsell, outmanage, outmotivate, and outnegotiate your competition. Knowing your customer means knowing what your customer really wants."

It's all about identifying the right decision-maker in a company and finding a hook to get in the door. Once in the door, it's all about building a relationship that will pay rewards when the company actually does have a project.

Don Erwin, veteran economic and commercial developer, says, there are three ways to get someone's undivided attention (In today's world one of the most precious things you can get.):

1. If the company decision-maker is from your state or community, was educated or lived or worked in your state or community,
2. If you know someone who knows the decision-maker and can make an introduction for you, and/or
3. If there are aspects of your state or community that the decision-maker admires, is attracted to, is connected to, or desires to participate in some way, e.g., likes to hunt, race cars, play golf, or vacation.[109]

But, it takes heavy-duty research to identify the prospects that fit these hooks and help open doors. A detailed client profile allows personalized responses and requests with information that

---

108 https://harveymackay.com/
109 Don Erwin Teaching Session, Applied Economic Development Honors' Class, 2019

indicates that you have gone beyond the basics on a client and his/her company. People love to hear their names and respond positively when they sense someone has taken the time to learn about them. Learning and remembering names and personal information is a gift for some but hard work for most. (Try repeating the name as soon as you hear it.)

Adapted from the *Mackay 66*, the following is a modified profile that fits the economic development world. In other words, try to get this information on each person/client to enhance your personalized communication and networking. (For more information about Harvey Mackay, go to www.harveymackay.com)

1. Name (Nickname)
2. Spouse name – occupation
3. Company name/address
4. Home address – will come in handy for certain invitations or personal notes
5. Basic contact information
6. Hometown/high school
   a. Any information on their upbringing – poor, middle-class or wealthy
7. Family background – connections through parents, brothers, sisters
   a. Interesting tidbits of information that can be used in face-to-face meetings or written communications
8. College – any interesting college life information that can be inserted in a future communication
9. Any connection to your state or community? Always useful information.
10. Children – names/ages/education
11. Previous employers – positions held – mainly for background but useful when discussing other companies
12. What boards do they serve on?

13. Political persuasion – which PACs do they contribute to?
14. Who do they associate with – friends, business people, politicians?
15. Lifestyle
    a. Does he/she drink? If not, offended by others drinking?
    b. Does he/she smoke? If not, objects to smoking?
    c. Does he/she use crude language? If not, you should watch your language in order not to offend (Probably a good idea anyway)
    d. Favorite restaurants
        i. Prefer breakfast, lunch, or dinner meetings
        ii. Favorite foods – might be useful at gift-giving time
        iii. Objects to or cannot have anyone buy their meal?
    e. Hobbies/recreational interests – always good when suggesting interaction opportunities
    f. Favorite vacation locations or types, e.g., RV, cruise, international, automotive
    g. Best conversational interests + **any issues to avoid**
    h. Does he/she have a close relationship with other communities or economic developers in your state/region?
    i. Past experiences – notes that might help future interactions

From this list of valuable client/prospect information one can readily see that prospect profiles take time and creativity to be effective. You can't just ask the client these questions so you must become a good observer, conversationalist, researcher, and spy. Of course, Google and LinkedIn are wonderful sources of information but conversations and just paying attention to the mementos and things in one's office can fill in much of the personal prospect profile form. There are other research sources (Wikipedia, Facebook, and Lexus/Nexus) that are also readily available. And, as technology and personal information expand, obtaining key bits of information toward effective marketing and interaction will be even easier.

Again, doing this right and keeping the information up to date is hard work – but work that will pay off many times over.

Direct Marketing

One of the most challenging aspects of economic development is targeted direct marketing. The keyword is **"targeted."** Initially, a community should determine what industry sectors best fit their assets based on three criteria:

1. People – what does my talent pipeline currently look like? But, also part of your thinking should be what my talent pipeline will look like in five, ten years.
2. Finance – what will my elected leaders and community support from an incentive standpoint?
3. Infrastructure – what assets are in place that will meet the needs of a target industry i.e. prepared/certified sites, available buildings, port, adequate runway, interstate access? Then ask the question, are our targets growing companies that, if attracted, will continue growth and expansion within the community, region, or state?

Too often, communities broaden the "targeted" industry list based on wishes not facts. The key is an honest assessment that narrows the focus to industry sectors that truly fit a community's profile. However, smart communities will also look toward growth sectors that fit the community as possible prospect leads.

This is not to say that the economic developer should not look down the road. In fact, the successful professional is thinking strategically ten years from now and identifying what new sectors might become targets if the community prepares properly. Once identified, these targets provide the beginning to building relationships with the people who match what the community wants to become.

Once a community determines the industry sectors that fit, the role of analytics comes into play. A data deep dive will reveal specific companies within a sector that fit the profile now. Then comes the task of learning about each targeted company and, most importantly, the best contact entry point into the company.

- Name of the company
- Key contact that makes sense – best entry point
- Assistant's name – quite often he/she is the gatekeeper that will unlock the door for a meeting.
- Contact's location and other company locations that might fit a visit
- Types of products produced, especially those that match your community's assets
- Suppliers, especially ones in your region – huge!
- How does your community compare to other locations through the eyes of a company decision-maker or site selection consultant that might represent the company in a site search – in essence, a competitive analysis to determine similar community traits
- Does the company already work with a site selection consultant? If yes, is the consultant the best entry point? The answer is probably yes so not to offend the consultant.
- Determine the best opportunity to visit – at a company site, trade show, or other event
- What type of visit? Introductory, social, conference, in-passing, virtual
- NOTE: After the visit always make notes ASAP, while fresh on your mind, to add to your prospect profile
- Follow-up materials – not boilerplate approach but really **listen** to what the prospect says and craft materials/responses that fit the situation they describe.

- Use the personal/professional information gleaned from visits/conversations as a reason for further contact, i.e., children's graduation, promotions, sports, etc.
- Consider others on your economic development team or in your community that might have entre' to this individual or the company, i.e., suppliers, banking connections, college connections, etc.

The key to effective targeted marketing is information that is gathered through a relentless pre-work process. The sports analogy comes into play. The successful teams do not begin their preparation on Saturday morning prior to that afternoon's football game. Prep begins months earlier through detailed information gathering about each opponent. So it is with successful economic development. Preparation is 90% of performance.

Your pre-work matters most when you are in front of the customer who is trying to decide. Starting, expanding, and locating a business are risky decisions. How do you reduce the customer's risk? Which aspects of a community/state matter the most to the profitable operation of the company's plant/operation/organization? Which aspects impact the quality of life desired? Pre-work means you know what to talk about with the presentation centering on their wants, needs, desires, and how they match with what the community has to offer. Confidence in speaking, knowledge of them and their business improves the community's chances of making the Final Few. As we have said often, it's all about preparation and homework.

It Does Matter What You Say

Too often, local economic developers approach dealing with the media in a hap-hazard manner and, unfortunately, pay a costly price. Effective working relations with news media can pay huge dividends and help the local organization establish a strong positive brand for the community. Or, a loose approach can bite you in the rear-end.

One training program thinks this subject is so important that they devote significant time to key lessons. The Advanced Economic Development Leadership Program, which was developed by five major universities, schedules a full day of effective media training and good speaking/presentation techniques.

When dealing with both the public and the media always consider the confidentiality balance required with active projects and applicable Sunshine laws in your state. An effective media strategy is a two-way street – both the interviewer and the one being interviewed have something to gain from good information and positive, accurate articles and TV segments. While the media may contact you on a particular issue, it can be advantageous to be proactive by pitching positive stories about job creation efforts in your community. In most cases, the local media, especially in smaller communities, recognize that they are part of the community fabric and will benefit from increased economic vitality.

Remember, one of the goals is to bring the community along in a shared economic development vision and the media can often be a vehicle to help accomplish this goal.

Lessons from Years in the Trenches

- Build good relationships with the local media in order to become their "go-to" economic development source – while you can always explain that you cannot comment because of XYZ, never just say "no comment".
- When a reporter calls, after determining the nature of the call, a good strategy might be to politely ask if you can call back in five minutes. This break allows time to carefully consider the best response and key points – make notes to ensure you use the right terms, phrases, and key points. In the back of your mind, picture what you would like tomorrow's headline to be based on your comments. Remember,

the reporter doesn't normally write the headline, so repeat key point(s) several times.

- For a television interview, think in terms of a ten to fifteen-second comment or soundbite – try to stick your key point in every response to ensure that the soundbite selected includes the main message.

- The old school approach is to interact with your media contact via telephone and, in the opinion of many, is still the best approach. However, if you do send a news release in advance, give the reporter a telephone call alerting them to expect the release and that you are available for follow-up.

- Sometimes the best approach on a particular story or issue is a face to face interview – often in their office or, in today's new normal, virtually. There is just something about looking each other in the eyes that strengthens the bond and allows a more positive interaction – and, hopefully, results in a better article or news story.

- If you are using an economic development volunteer, local expert, or elected official as the spokesperson or participant in the interview, be sure to prep them. Prep them well, often with mock Q&A sessions, so they are prepared with appropriate statements and possible responses to expected and unexpected questions. Everyone on your team involved in an interview needs to be on the same page – have the same talking points. In all cases, when using a spokesperson other than the economic developer, the professional needs to be the quarterback. In other words, the QB sets the interview and always sits in as another pair of eyes and ears – and, just in case clarification on a particular point is necessary in follow-up.

Countless books, articles, and speeches have outlined the secrets to good media relations. But, in the end, recognizing that the media has a job to do just as those in the economic development profession is a great first step in a good, working relationship. There is also an old adage that you never ever lie to the media because of the obvious consequences but also because it can destroy the trust level developed over many years of hard work. And thirdly, know when to fight or most likely, avoid a fight, with someone who buys ink by the barrel or with television, who has the last word.

Building good media relations takes work, honesty, and transparency. The following are more key lessons on today's news media that may help prepare you for successful interaction.

- **Over the years, soundbites have shrunk.** In 1960, a presidential candidate could expect around 45 seconds of what he said to be aired on the evening news. Now, with the explosion of cable and local news, reporters prefer 6-12 second answers to their questions. The burden for the interviewee is to prepare and then answer questions succinctly to avoid being interrupted or edited. A good interview is 90% preparation.
- **Today, everyone is a potential reporter.** Cell phones, YouTube, and other instant sources make casual comments potentially news making. It is extremely important to watch what you say in public gatherings or discussions.
- **Newspapers still have a role, especially in rural America.** Large newspaper readership may be declining in big cities, but local newspapers still set the news agenda in many communities. Get to know print reporters and cultivate a positive business relationship. Newspapers have the inherent space to go into more depth than television or radio so prepare differently for television where visuals can be a powerful tool.
- **The Ammerman Experience lists four steps to succeed with the news media**[110]:

---

110 https://ammermanexperience.com/

- ○ **Control**: A successful media interview is about preparation and control. It's about getting your message across rather than hoping it will happen by itself.
- ○ **Confidence**: Be confident – if you are afraid or nervous, you probably won't be at your best. Confidence results from good prep, subject knowledge, practice, and experience.[111]
- ○ **Connection**: Try to establish a link between you and the reporter so you have a better chance to connect with the viewing audience
- ○ **Credibility**: You've got to make me believe that you believe what you are saying before I can also believe. Confusing, but a simple truth. Always stick to the truth and the facts as the first step toward establishing credibility and believability.
- **What's the subject for the interview?** Establish that before you agree to the interview. Plan to use the interview wisely by jotting down three points you want to make and keep inserting a key point with each answer to ensure the chances of getting your points in print and on the air.
- **90% of success is preparation**: To craft a strong message or key point, think like a reporter. Expect to be asked the proverbial: Who? What? When? Where? How? How much? Remember, the well-known scouting motto still works.
- **Listen – Think – Respond**: A successful interview or Q&A following a news conference requires concentration. Listen and concentrate on the entire question. Don't formulate your answer without hearing the entire question. It's a courtesy as well as smart business.

---

111 Confidence means being able to summon your talent and skill when the outcome is on the line. Believe it or not, your love for what you do drives your ability to sink the free throw when the National Championship is on the line. You have got to want the ball. You need confidence in sales too.

- **The Bridging Technique**: Most media trainers, including Ken Haseley of The Ammerman Experience, spend a lot of time discussing the technique to get back to the talking points you prepared for the interview. In his book, *You Are the Message*,[112] controversial media expert Roger Ailes gave the equation, $Q = A + 1$, in which Q represents the reporter's question, A is your answer to the question and $+1$ represents the bridge to your key point – something like this:
  - ° Q: Don't most people consider these incentives for Project X to be corporate welfare?
  - ° A: I have no way of knowing...
  - ° +1: But what I do know is that we prepared a comprehensive cost-benefit analysis for the City Council and the local investment in this project will create ___ jobs, provide excellent skills training, and a positive financial benefit to businesses across the community.
- **Bridging Language**: The Ammerman Experience's Ken Haseley says try these bridging statements to get to your talking points:
  - ° What's more important is...
  - ° The most important thing...
  - ° Here's another way to say it...
  - ° What's important for people to know is...
  - ° Let's talk about...
- **Avoid personal opinions**: You are not being interviewed because of your private views so keep your opinions to yourself. Remember, what you say could be the headline tomorrow morning.
- **Speculation**: Engaging in hypothetical or speculative banter with an interviewer is dangerous and one you cannot win. Avoid "what if" questions.

---

112 Roger Ailes and Jon Kraushar, *You Are the Message: Getting What You Want by Being Who You Are*, December 1995, Doubleday Books.

- **Off the record**: "Can we go off the record?" Almost every time you make that suggestion, it doesn't work so avoid going there. There are instances where certain trustworthy reporters will honor information on "background only" but always be careful.

- **Blind Source**: This one can sneak up on you. If the reporter quotes a memo, article, or comment from an unnamed source, don't go there either. Ask to see it and respond only after you've had ample time to review in order to frame an adequate response.

- **No Comment**: The phrase "no comment" implies you are evading the issue, hiding something or your organization is guilty of some wrongdoing or shady actions. NEVER say "no comment." Instead, give sound reasons why you will not or cannot answer the question. In the economic development business, a Non-Disclosure Agreement (NDA) with the client; "still under negotiation;" proprietary information; pending litigation or lack of authority to address that issue can all be good but correct responses to a question that you cannot answer.

- **Negatives**: Unfortunately, most news today is negative because, as they say, "it sells newspapers." Why did you agree to these outrageous incentives? What happens if the company doesn't perform per the agreement? Who's at fault? As a result, reporters frequently employ negative phrases in their questioning. **Don't repeat** them in your answer. Some classic interviewees have even injected them into their own statements. Seasoned readers may remember Richard Nixon's classic self-inflicted wound – "The American public needs to know whether their president is a crook. Well, I am not a crook."[113]

---

113 Richard Nixon, *Checker's Speech*, November 17, 1973

- **Silence can be deadly, not golden**: Americans have an issue with silence – it's awkward and we don't like it. But, in an interview, avoid the temptation to keep talking once you've finished your statement. Good reporters often remain silent hoping you will keep talking once you've finished your prepared comments. If you must speak, use the silence to go back to your key point. And, always, always assume that a microphone is live, even after the interview. Very polished interviewees have been caught saying things after an interview that made the news that they wish had never been spoken.
- **Guarantees**: If a reporter asks if you can guarantee something (e.g. the company will hire the employees they've announced), avoid saying "No, I can't guarantee that" or similar responses. Tomorrow's headline will probably be "EDA Cannot Guarantee Announced Jobs." Instead, using the bridge technique say, "What I can guarantee is…" Then fill in with a statement that is positive and more comfortable. In prep time, try to anticipate negative questions so everyone being interviewed is prepared with a good bridge and positive answer.
- **The Seat of Human Emotion**: if you want to get your message across to the listener or reader, you must reach and connect with their seat of human emotion. You must convince this part of the listener's brain that you are trustworthy, believable, credible, and yes, even likable.

Presentations and Speeches Can Pay Off Handsomely
Developing good media relations is very important for those times of interaction with the working press. In the same context, public speaking or presentations are an important aspect of a successful economic development strategy. We all think we're pretty good communicators, but the truth is most of us are not nearly as good as we think.

It may be in front of the city council requesting incentives for a new project, briefing your stakeholders on the EDA, speaking to the local civic club, or preparing your local team for the next prospect visit, but presentations say much about the ability to effectively communicate a message and the credibility of the message itself.

All have endured bad presentations or daydreamed during a particularly boring speech. Every economic developer should experience speech/presentation training at some point to hone their communication skills.

Some face an upcoming presentation with excitement while others compare it to going to the dentist. But, in most cases, it is a necessary part of many job descriptions, and quite often, is a wonderful time to influence people and decision-makers.

Let's look at eight rules that will help effectively communicate your message:

- Be excited about the opportunity – the audience can sense when you're "not feeling it" and will lose interest early in the presentation – studies show it takes **8 seconds** to lose someone's attention. Consider beginning with questions to engage the audience.
- Research the audience before you speak – don't use boilerplate speeches – make sure your presentation is relevant to the audience. When the time comes for the speech or even while you're waiting at the head table for showtime, read the audience and adjust on the fly if necessary. Too many speakers drone on with their prepared remarks no matter what. Be prepared to adapt on the fly.
- Have a key point in mind that you want to communicate and indicate that message early and often (creatively, of course). Try not to prepare a speech but instead develop your outline and key point based on understanding the audience's needs. Reading a speech negates most of the

opportunity to connect with the audience – eye to eye contact works. Use it.

- Body language is important – again, the audience can sense if you are friend or foe, interesting or dull – look people in the eye – become adept at understanding the unspoken body language of your audience because the greatest wealth of acceptance or rejection lie's in people's body language. You must pay attention to what *isn't* said more than what *is* said to discover their true feelings. For instance, if you see them yawning or working the cell phone, try to move to a more interesting point or a story to illustrate the key message, even ask a question.

- Be careful with visual aids – stay away from texts on the screen and only use visuals that will reinforce your key points. Remember, you want them to focus on you and your comments and complicated slides with too much information break their focus on the real message. Think about effective billboards[114] and use only enough words to communicate or tease.

- In some settings, find a way to engage or interact with the audience. Get them involved in your presentation but do so creatively. You might test an exercise with your staff to get their reaction and either continue, adapt, or discard.

- The Lord gave us one mouth and two ears for a purpose – listen more than you talk during the question/answer session. Make it clear that you hear what the person is saying. Reframe what you heard to make sure of your understanding and avoid thinking about your response while they are still speaking (Guilty). It's OK to ask questions but don't

---

114 The best billboards are the ones the billboard sign company uses to advertise their billboard business. An attention capturing image with very few words. Mimic them.

interrupt. Again, your body language will tip off your true reaction.

- End early rather than late! Try to leave time for questions and discussion.

Take Communication Seriously

Reading about effective speaking and good media relations is only part of the equation. You must practice and practice some more. Make practice a part of your teams' professional development which might include making the speech or presentation in front of your staff (and a mirror as well)! There is an old saying that practice makes perfect. Perhaps the better saying is "Perfect Practice Makes Perfect."

Take your communication strategy seriously and it will pay dividends for you, your organization, and, more importantly, your community.

CHAPTER 15
FINISH WELL

"The two most important days of your life are the day
that you were born and the day you found out why"
—*Mark Twain*

The morning sun rose as the team prepared for a day that would cul-
minate in delivering Project Penguin to the site consultant. David
had been at the office since six reviewing the response between sips
of dark magic coffee and Fiber One bars. As the team gathered two
hours later for a final session, the Keurig operated on overtime and
everyone was tempted by Dunkin Donuts that Adrienne brought to
the party.

The team could sense they had a strong proposal and felt they
would soon be hosting the company's decision-makers in Bedford
for the final phase of the competition. It wasn't a cocky attitude, but
one based on confidence that they hadn't left anything on the field.
It was a good feeling.

In the back of their minds, they knew Bedford was the perfect site for the company and they could be the partner that
would get the company up and running in record time. It would
be a life-changer for both the economic development team and

the community. Some of their neighbors and people they had never met would have jobs that would change their lives. All the blood, sweat, and tears that led to this final session would be worth it.

They had to remind themselves not to get ahead of the process — it's not over until it's over. But they were proud of their work and would sleep well tonight knowing they had crafted a first-class proposal. Now it was up to the Project Penguin decision-maker. Tomorrow the Bedford EDA team would focus on the pandemic recovery, a few other new challenges, and catch up on ones that had taken a momentary back seat like the marketing revision. It's what made them look forward to the unscripted, exciting days that lay ahead knowing they would be impacting people's lives in every action they took.

E conomic development can be fast-paced, high stress, demanding career choice. It can also be very rewarding when the folks you live and work around find enhanced opportunities for better-paying jobs.

There is a time for everything and a season for every activity under heaven

—*Ecclesiastes 3:1*

It can be all-consuming just as with any career choice. Interviews with professional economic developers caution about finding balance in the pressure cooker world of job creation. As with other stressful jobs, it can produce burnout and fatigue especially in those early career years when one is trying to establish themselves as the best and brightest.

The same can be said for elected officials who enter the political ring with high hopes and dreams for their communities but quickly learn the realities of local public service. Every elected official that puts his/her name on the ballot deserves respect for their willingness to serve the people.

A time to be born and a time to die, a time to plant and a time to uproot

—Ecclesiastes 3:2

Life is very much a balancing act. We are constantly trying to move forward with purpose, achieve goals, and not neglect family time all the while walking a tightrope suspended fifty feet above a straw-covered floor - trying to keep it all in perfect alignment to avoid cascading downward.

Warren Bennis, one of the country's leadership experts, wrote, "No leader sets out to be a leader. People set out to live their lives, expressing themselves fully. When that expression is of value, they become leaders. So, the point is not to become a leader. The point is to become yourself, to use yourself completely – all your skills, gifts, and energies – in order to make your vision manifest. You must withhold nothing. You must, in sum, become the person you started out to be and enjoy the process of becoming."[115]

Through the process of "becoming," we have to balance so many things in our lives – work, family, leisure, play, caring for others, spiritual growth, internal politics, and physical needs. Finding balance in our lives is so important to healthy, active, productive work, and private lives. Actually, finding balance is a lifetime pursuit. It is ongoing and a process. It's about finding a quality of life that balances all that is important to you.

---

115 Warren Bennis, *On Becoming a Leader*, 1989, Perseus Books Group.

A time to scatter stones and a time to gather them, a time to embrace and a time to refrain, a time to search and a time to give up, a time to keep and a time to throw away

—*Ecclesiastes 3:5*

Samantha Stosur says that "tennis is all about mental toughness and you have to keep your head in the game. I make time to relax away from competition pressures, travel, and intense training' schedules to make sure I'm looking after myself. Taking time out with family and friends helps to maintain the work-life balance everyone needs."[116]

So, where do those charged with bringing new wealth and jobs to our communities begin? Is a healthy balance possible? Let's slow down and follow Jimmy Buffett's advice – Breathe In, Breathe Out, Move On.

- A balanced life is not the end goal but an ongoing process. You don't achieve it at the end of your career but every day. And throughout the process there will be stumbles coupled with moments of great euphoria. It's a mindset that each of us makes a conscious decision that **balance** enhances every aspect of our life.
- Assess your life as it is now while incorporating continuous improvement into the process. Today is the starting point which allows you to reassess yourself continuously. It's a conscious process involving honest evaluation. Am I tilted one way too much and not enough in another way?
- Everyone should set goals for the key areas of their lives. Goal setting will require prioritization within these key areas:
  - ° Your spiritual life
  - ° Your family
  - ° Your job

---

116 https://www.pinterest.com/pin/507358714246682806/

- ° Your relationships and friends
- ° Your physical well being
- ° Your finances

It is often difficult to rank the list in a proper order because decisions happen daily. The millennial society and, honestly some of the older generation, are addicted to social media. Finding balance might start as simply as whether to check emails or carry on a conversation with your oldest child sans smartphone.

- It takes discipline to decide what is important, focus on it, and get it done. Today, many more people have been forced to work from home due to COVID requiring new disciplines and regimens. Finding balance can enhance the effectiveness of one's discipline and priority alignment. Finding balance can enhance one's discipline.
- We are all tempted to ease back into comfortable routines. Be specific about daily, even hourly, decisions. We tend to generalize and say we're going to spend more quality time with our children or eat healthier or exercise or study my Bible or visit with friends. All are generalizations that may or may not happen. Be specific with an actual schedule.
- Finding balance means delegating responsibilities. If you're bearing the load at work or at home, you're not balanced. Or, if you're not carrying your share of the load there cannot be balance either. Strength and growth come from interacting, learning from the person in the next office, and debating the right course of action. Recognize others have strengths they can share, reducing the burdens of the office or home. In *Remembering the Titans*[117], during a time of racial unrest, the established white coach that felt he should

---

117 *Remember the Titans* Walt Disney Pictures, 2000, written by Gregory Allen Howard, directed by Boaz Yakin

have had the head coaching job finally had to admit that he needed help coaching the linemen from the new African American head coach. He recognized his limitations and the strengths someone else brought to the team. Together, they produced a championship football program.

- A good process promises success. Don't mentally skip to the end result but focus on the intermediate daily/weekly steps that fulfill a realistic, productive process toward an end game. "I need to get in shape" which is the end result. But in the short term, on a daily or weekly basis, I'm going to do certain manageable things toward that goal. We can get our arms around those snackable steps.
- There is an old saying that you can learn more from your failures than your successes. Both are part of life and have roles to play in developing a balanced life. We all enjoy being on top of the mountain, but appreciation for the pinnacle comes from our experiences in the valley. Failure is a part of economic development and, if used properly, can prepare us for that awesome triumph – that is, if we learn the valuable lessons from defeat.
- Finding balance includes quiet time to reflect and assess. We have to make time to reassess our situation – private time for yourself includes honest reflection. It may be thoughtful assessment or a review of written goals and processes or just the opportunity to think through a challenging situation. Strong coffee and a quiet corner can often allow the meditative juices to rebalance the edges that too often get off-kilter.
- As a change agent or economic development disrupter, it is important to focus on both the strengths and weaknesses of your environs. We often spend too much time on what's wrong and don't appreciate what's right. Good change agents can discern where to focus their attention – what is

doable and what will have the desired impact on my community? The ultimate goal is to develop wisdom to know where to focus attention, action, and inclusion.

At the end of the day, we often think back on whether we were successful or not. It can also include a reflection on stages in our lives. As agents of economic development, are we really making a difference in the world around us? Do we see success in final terms or as ongoing?

A time to tear and a time to mend, a time to be silent and a time to speak.

—Ecclesiastes 3:7

In her book, *Reach for the Summit,* former Tennessee basketball Coach Pat Summit wrote, "There are different kinds of success. There is fame and fortune, which…is a pretty flimsy, short-lived kind of success. Then there is the more gratifying kind of success that comes from doing something you love and doing it well. Still another kind of success results from committing to one person and raising a child with them. Yet another is finding a sustained faith in your church. But notice something about all the various forms of success. They are **open-ended.** They aren't tasks that you finish. Success is a project that's always under construction. Somehow, you have to make a commitment to get better every day, no matter how successful you were the day before."[118]

Pat Summit nails it! When the nightfall comes following a long arduous fight to win a major new project and the excitement fades from the afternoon's announcement, reality sets in the next morning that the process begins all over again with a whole new set of

---

118 *Reach for the Summit,* Pat Summitt with Sally Jenkins, 1998, Random House, NY.

challenges and opportunities. Successful economic development is always under construction. And, that's what makes it an exciting and challenging profession.

Let us run with endurance the race set before
us…rather than chasing after the wind.

—*Hebrews 12:1-2*

APPENDIX

The Role of the Economic Development Quarterback

The future is not some place we are going. It is the place we, the community, create with our decisions and actions.

Successful community economic development requires a team of involved individuals and organizations led by a quarterback – the professional leader of the economic development organization. Early on individual political leaders aided by volunteers and their combined political connections were behind the progress we saw in local economies. Although the role played by political leaders has not diminished in importance, over time, the growth of knowledgeable location customers from all over the globe accompanied with their consultants and the resulting intensive competitiveness between alternate location offerings made the need for full-time professional practitioners to lead a community, state, or region imperative. With increased competition, final deal complexity increased geometrically, and all communities needed professional economic developers to lead their efforts.

Throughout this growth and change, the objective of the economic development process stayed the same – create new wealth and a higher standard of living in the community, state, or region served. Lately we added sustainable growth to the mantra.

To remain competitive, economic development professionals must continue to learn and adapt to handle the complexities of modern economic development practice. The following list covers some of their common responsibilities regardless of location. Please note, many professionals do more than these. Few do less. In addition to meeting the requirements of the previous list (see page 17) of potential customers, success requires these professionals to:

1. Build/Maintain an intensely competitive, and in some cases a global, organization requiring input and resources from a diverse group of community and statewide stakeholders.
    a. Interact with supervising Board(s) and their organizations – create vision, monitor, and approve actions.
    b. Build an organizational culture that values learning, building expertise, and being adaptive to changes. Employees, and others, look to the quarterback to make sense of the business world, the community, and state as they are now. This requires direct contact with people in the marketplace and the courage to see things with an open mind.
    c. A community of constituents who substantially participate in the process of changing the fundamental structure of their local economy. This means the community is ready for economic development. Therefore, citizens must make the connection between a successful job creation/retention program and the resulting new wealth that trickles down throughout the community. The typical reaction in local media to economic development news gives an indication if the community

stakeholders complete the mental bridge that connects the EDO's activities with the rise in per capita income. Unfortunately, in many locations, this mental bridge is not complete, so media coverage needs attention.

    d. An involved group of allies (force multipliers) who are actively engaged in assisting the accomplishment of the organization's goals. Here is a list:

        i. State and Local Elected Officials and their Appointees and Organizations;

        ii. Electric, Gas, Communication Infrastructure (Telephone, Cable, & High-Speed Internet), Real Estate, Banking, and Logistic Suppliers;

        iii. Workforce Development – Public Education, Technical School, College and University; and

        iv. Key Community, Individuals, and Business Organizations (Each independently and/or collectively) and especially the local media[119].

2. Be able to understand, lead, and handle all dealings with:

    a. Prospects from the local area served, throughout America and the globe. Economic developers meet their goals by appealing to entrepreneurs[120] as well as new and existing businesses who are looking for a new location or thinking about expanding or leaving one.

    b. Their own organization – employees and volunteers engaging in the actual process of utilizing the known (land, workforce, infrastructure, resources, entrepreneurism, tax revenue, and all of the above) and sometimes unknown assets and resources (because customer

---

119 Yes, the media can be a friend and an advocate. See guidelines for interacting with the media under sub-heading *Lessons from Years in the Trenches*, beginning near the bottom on Page 107.

120 It may come as a surprise to some, but new wealth creation is much more than job recruitment or attraction.

requirements change) in a community, state or region to grow the economy.

3. Analyze Target Industry Data and Select Industry/Company Focus, Establish Strategic Priorities, Align Resources, Build Strategies and Plans including Goals, Measure Results, and Be Prepared to Take Corrective Action. The Business for Social Responsibility lists five core principles for a successful community and economic development:

   a. Be strategic,
   b. Adopt a community-driven focus,
   c. Build capacity which provides for the businesses we create, attract, retain, or expand (CARE)[121],
   d. Work in partnership, and
   e. Design for sustainability, characterized by the 1987 Brundtland Report which defined sustainable development as, "that which meets the needs of the community in the present without compromising the future".[122]

4. Handle the pressure -- often the challenge for the economic development professional is to manage the pressure from elected officials and stakeholders which quite often is: What have you done for me lately?

Thank You for reading all the way to the end.

Your questions and comments are always welcome:
N.Wade@usm.edu
Bill.Smith@usm.edu

---

121   CARE acronym used at University of Southern Mississippi Masters in Economic Development program.

122   From Chapter 2 - *Towards Sustainable Development*, page 54, 1987 Brundtland Report, United Nations World Commission on Environment and Development. https://en.wikisource.org/wiki/Brundtland_Report/Chapter_2._Towards_Sustainable_Development

GLOSSARY

Alliance: formal arrangement between two or more entities for ongoing cooperation and mutual gain.

Application: putting into practice accumulated knowledge; not enough to know, it must be applied to be effective.

Branding: process of creating a unique image that defines a community/state in the customer's mind; one's marketing brand message must sync in the minds of the decision-makers.

Brownfield Site: real property where potential development is impacted or impeded by the presence of hazardous pollutants or contaminated materials.

Business Attraction/Recruitment: a key traditional strategy by communities/states to induce industries/businesses from outside the area to locate inside the region/state.

Business Retention/Expansion (BRE): a key leg in the job creation stool where communities proactively connect with existing businesses to strengthen and maintain good relationships which encourages wealth creation from within existing companies in the community/region.

CARE: acronym for the four ways to grow and sustain an economy: **Create, Attract, Retain, Expand**.

Change: is a given. It will happen. Your community or economic development organization will either **adapt, decline, or possibly die**.

Change Agent: one willing to assess and determine what needs to be changed in a community to achieve success and then acts.

Clawbacks: a part of a local/state incentive package establishing punitive financial steps or paybacks against companies that do not meet job creation and investment commitments; a provision that makes sure taxpayer subsidies pay off. May involve renegotiation due to external events, e.g., Covid-19.

Community Development: process of people working together to solve common problems that impede job and economic growth; getting a community primed for economic growth.

Community Vitality Index or DNA: a realistic view of a community based on key competition pillars; process that looks inside each unique community to define the unique characteristics impacting economic development competitiveness.

Coopetition: when community competitors cooperate in certain efforts, i.e., marketing strategies knowing they will also compete in the site selection marketplace.

Corporate Welfare: critics often refer to local/state incentives as corporate welfare.

Cost-Benefit Analysis: method to evaluate and justify a proposed incentive package especially pertaining to government incentive decisions; study to show when an incentivized project pays off.

Disruptive Economic Development: almost always includes rethinking challenges, vision strategies, and redefining what is around you – creating new options for economic growth; not accepting the status quo.

Economic Development: process of creating new wealth; process of elimination in site selection.

Economic Gardening: focused growth from within a community i.e. entrepreneurs and nurturing local businesses.

Economic Leakage: Capital or citizen's income that exits a community rather than being spent inside a community or region.

Entrepreneur: someone who starts a business and is willing to take risks to be successful: a growing important sector in a local job creation strategy.

Final Few: inside the site selection process of elimination, the three of four finalist communities for project selection; what every competitive community should be striving to attain.

Force Multipliers: individuals and organizations who expand the community's job creation reach to influencers, expertise, and prospects; fulfill prospect demand and have the capability to multiply budgets.

Gatekeeper: someone who stands between you and the decision-maker; often those successful in a community and satisfied with its status quo and do not want to see change, growth, and higher wages.

Greenfield: land not previously developed or prepared for development.

Incentives: financial, in-kind community benefits offered as part of a strategy to win a new project or business expansion, e.g., tax abatements, tax credits, infrastructure improvements, cash inducements, job training.

Impact Analysis: a model to analyze positive and negative impacts expected from a prospective new industry/business on a community.

Industry Cluster: grouping of similar industries and suppliers within a geographic area to increase productivity, economies, and profitability.

Job Tax Credit: A credit on taxes owed that can be used to reduce the state income tax liability of a business/industry; often part of a state or local community incentive package.

Jobs Created Definition:

- **Direct Jobs** – direct employment at a plant or business within the community
- **Indirect Jobs** – as a result of direct jobs, additional workers are generated at businesses that supply goods or services to the main plant i.e. suppliers
- **Induced Jobs** – new jobs created as a result of employees spending their wages in local businesses, restaurants, etc.

Labor Shed: geographic area from which an industry or business can recruit workers based on commuting patterns, population, and workforce availability.

Leaderfulness: every facet of the community is involved in the economic growth process and the steps to improve community competitiveness.

Leadership: an influence process toward a particular goal or outcome; leader effectiveness depends on understanding those you want to influence, their ability to grasp the commitment, and providing encouragement throughout the process.

Marketing: strategic process of promoting the benefits of a community/state to targeted business/industry decision-makers based upon understanding Customer needs and desires first. Marketing is best considered a philosophy, a method of thinking meant to guide action.

Multiplier Effect: total employment created for every basic employee created at the potential/local plant, e.g., in an automotive assembly plant the typical multiplier is about 5 to 1 – therefore, for every direct job another four indirect/induced jobs will be created.

New Market Tax Credits: Incentives for investment in low-income communities. Investors receive a tax credit against their Federal income tax; a congressionally authorized incentive program.

One-Stop Shop or Permitting: a central permitting destination designed to ease the process in a timely and efficient manner for effectiveness; reality must meet branding claims.

Operating Budget: Budget established and approved for the operation of an economic development organization.

Per Capita Income: the average income earned per person in a specified area or region. Calculated by dividing an area's total income by its total population.

Prepared Community: hard, continuous improvement process that requires constant review, action, and necessary local due diligence with appropriate improvement actions.

Preponderance of Evidence: the proving process that many site consultants require re: community/state claims especially statements about the availability of workforce excellence; community must present evidence that the claim is more probable than not.

Pro-Business Environment: climate that is good for and supportive of local businesses; stable economy, fair and timely regulation, supportive elected officials, adequate infrastructure, and local amenities.

Process: a good process produces good results and requires an owner.

Prospect Sequence: a lead > prospect > projects > Final Few > Selection

Quality of Life: the level of health, education, leisure, happiness, prosperity, safety experienced with a community; general well-being and expectations for a good life and successful business.

Quarterback: in the job creation world, preferably the professional lead economic developer.

Request for Information (RFI): first step in the site selection process to gather data and specific information related to a possible project; coveted by all economic development organizations.

Request for Proposal (RFP): Even more coveted by economic development organizations; your community has been invited to enter the site competition for a project.

Rural: defined as open country with populations less than 2,500; any population not in an urban area; Wikipedia defines rural as located outside towns/cities. (Editor's note: some books have defined rural as off the interstates. Many smaller cities do themselves a disservice by describing themselves as a rural community. We tend to believe these community's and small cities are America's Heartland)

Shovel-Ready Sites: ready for development; can be built upon immediately; completed due diligence and fully vetted including zoning, surveys, title work, environmental, soil analysis, utilities, and necessary public infrastructure.

Site Certification: a third-party seal of approval that a site has proper due diligence and is ready for development.

Site Selector: also known as a site eliminator; key point of contact hired by a company to identify potential locations for new or expanded development.

Skills Gap: difference between the skills required for a job vs. skills local workforce candidate(s) actually possess.

Skills Mismatch: situation in which jobs are available but cannot be filled due to a lack of workforce candidates' necessary or required skills.

Spec Building: a building shell that can easily be converted into a prospective company-specific requirement.

Start-up: first stage in creation of business; very iffy for local/state cash incentive.

Strategic Economic Development Plan: process to develop a clear vision for the community, set of goals to reach the vision, strategies to achieve each goal, implementation schedule, and evaluation of process.

Sustainable Development: conducted with protection of natural resources; job creation while sustaining natural resources and ecosystems; does not compromise future generations' needs.

SWOT Analysis: Strengths, Weaknesses, Opportunities, Threats within a community/region; how is a community leveraging assets/resources vs. mitigating risks and threats?

Targeted: the industry/business sectors that best fit a community's assets; an honest assessment of assets rather than through rose-colored glasses.

Tax Increment Financing (TIF): WHOOPS Allocates future increases in property taxes from a designated area to pay for improvements within that defined area. It is usually triggered based on the investment by the project and the size of the proposed site.

Tax Abatement: exemption or reduction in tax liability in exchange for specified new job creation and investment.

Under-Employed: all persons with higher skills or credentials than required for the job they presently hold.

Unemployed: all working-age persons not able to find a job but desiring full-time work; do not have a job, actively looking for employment for the prior four weeks.

Values: What you stand for! What you demand from your team – your standard of operation.

Value Proposition: the value an economic development organization promises to bring its funding partners, governmental entities, and stakeholders; why a business or government should invest in the EDA. What the community/state is offering the potential and existing businesses they interact with.

Vision Statement: a guide for the organization to make decisions that align with its goals; what business are you in; a preferred picture of the future.

INDEX

Made in the USA
Las Vegas, NV
19 August 2021

28463379R00115